The Ayurveda Cookbook for Women

Regain Emotional Balance and Take Control
of Your Health Through the Ayurvedic Culinary Remedies.
Including 100+ Recipes to Support Your Holistic Wellness

By
Sameera B. Joyce

Table of Contents

Soups and Salads   75

Main Courses   91

Introduction

Welcome to The Ayurveda Cookbook for Women 2024, a culinary journey that explores the ancient wisdom of Ayurveda and its profound impact on women's health and well-being. My name is Sameera B. Joyce, and I am delighted to be your guide on this transformative adventure. Having grown up in India, I have always been fascinated by the rich traditions and healing properties of Ayurveda. Through my travels and culinary explorations, I have discovered the immense power of food to nourish, heal, and bring balance to our lives.

This cookbook is designed with women in mind, providing a collection of over 150 mouthwatering recipes that celebrate the wisdom of Ayurveda and its potential to support our unique health and well-being needs. The book is divided into four chapters, each dedicated to a key aspect of Ayurvedic living: understanding Ayurvedic principles, embracing the Ayurvedic lifestyle, building a healthy Ayurvedic kitchen, and finally, the delicious recipes themselves.

The first chapter delves into the fundamental principles of Ayurveda, including the three doshas, the Ayurvedic approach to nutrition and cooking, seasonal eating, and the mind-body connection. By understanding these core principles, you will be better equipped to make informed choices about the food you consume, ensuring that it nourishes and supports your unique body type and constitution.

In the second chapter, we will explore the many ways in which you can integrate the principles of Ayurveda into your daily life, from meal planning and preparation to working with an Ayurvedic practitioner. This chapter also provides an overview of how Ayurveda fits into modern health and wellness trends and how it can be combined with other healing modalities for optimal results.

The third chapter focuses on building a healthy Ayurvedic kitchen, covering essential ingredients and spices, cooking techniques, and kitchen tools and equipment. This knowledge will empower you to create nourishing and flavorful dishes that honor the principles of Ayurveda and support your overall health and well-being.

Finally, the fourth chapter presents an array of delectable recipes, organized by meal type and including breakfasts, appetizers, soups, salads, main courses, sides, desserts, and beverages. Each recipe has been carefully crafted to provide a balance of flavors and nutrients that cater to the specific needs of women.

By incorporating Ayurvedic principles into your daily life and embracing a more mindful and holistic approach to health and nutrition, you can support your unique needs and promote overall health and happiness, both in and out of the kitchen. My hope is that this cookbook empowers you with the knowledge and tools you need to take charge of your health and well-being and inspires you to make Ayurvedic principles a part of your daily life.

So, let's embark on this exciting journey together, as we uncover the secrets of Ayurveda and learn to nourish our bodies, minds, and spirits with the wisdom of this ancient healing tradition. I invite you to savor each recipe, experiment with new flavors and ingredients, and most importantly, enjoy the process of self-discovery and growth that comes with embracing the Ayurvedic way of life.

With love and gratitude,

Sameera B. Joyce

CHAPTER 1

Understanding Ayurvedic Principles

Ayurvedic culinary practices extend beyond merely creating dishes in the kitchen—it encompasses an entire way of living. This book's recipe section will guide you towards embracing an Ayurvedic diet and lifestyle. The recipes serve as a starting point, but the primary goal is to teach you how to incorporate Ayurvedic principles into your cooking and daily routine. This concept involves preparing fresh meals for yourself, adhering to a seasonal eating pattern, and maintaining regular meal times. The following suggestions will assist you in focusing on aspects of your diet that are less about the specific foods and more about food's overall role in your life.

Ayurvedic eating considers intention, attitude, time of day, meal vs. snack distinction, portion size, season, and the dining environment. In this chapter, you'll find practical advice for each of these facets, allowing you to explore new perspectives on food. To ensure a smooth transition, start with one or two tips that resonate with you instead of attempting to implement all at once. Gradual change helps maintain stability in the body and mind, while trying to achieve too much too quickly can lead to burnout.

The Three Doshas

Most individuals acquainted with Ayurveda have heard of the doshas. Dosha, which literally means "that which is at fault," is not problematic until an imbalance lingers in the body for an extended period. These energies can be beneficial or harmful, depending on their relative balance. Therefore, it is more crucial to understand how to maintain equilibrium than to focus on doshas as villains.

There are three doshas—vata, pitta, and kapha—that arise when the five elements combine in specific proportions to form a human organism. Each dosha performs a distinct function in the body and exhibits a unique set of qualities.

· VATA (VA-tah) is the energy of movement.

· PITTA (PITT-ah) is the energy of transformation.

· KAPHA (CUP-hah) is the energy of structure, lubrication, and cohesion.

At the heart of Ayurveda, the ancient Indian system of holistic wellness, lies the concept of the three doshas: vata, pitta, and kapha. These doshas represent the unique combinations of the five elements – space, air, fire, water, and earth – and play a crucial role in shaping our physical, mental, and emotional well-being. By understanding the three doshas and their unique characteristics, we can uncover the keys to achieving balance, harmony, and vibrant health.

VATA

Vata dosha is formed by the elements of space and air, giving rise to qualities like cold, light, dry, rough, mobile, and erratic. Vata is responsible for all movement within the body, including circulation, respiration, and communication between cells. It also governs the functions of the nervous system, controlling cognitive abilities like creativity, intuition, and mental flexibility.

When vata is in balance, it supports regular elimination, easy breathing, proper circulation, and sharp senses. However, an imbalance of vata qualities can lead to gas and constipation, difficulty breathing, cold extremities, and feelings of anxiety or being overwhelmed.

How to balance Vata dosha

Harmonizing the Vata dosha by focusing on rejuvenating, warming, and stabilizing habits:

· Consume warm, moist foods high in protein and fat, featuring sweet, sour, and salty flavors while avoiding dry and cold items like dehydrated fruits and frozen treats.

- Establish consistent daily routines for eating, hydrating (particularly vital for this air-based dosha, which heightens dryness), meditating, and sleeping.
- Steer clear of irregular or chaotic schedules, limit travel, and reduce time spent using technology. Introducing regularity is essential for this dosha's balance.

PITTA

Pitta dosha is a combination of fire and water elements, resulting in qualities such as hot, light, slightly oily, sharp, and penetrating. Pitta governs transformation, metabolism, and digestion within the body. It is responsible for breaking down and assimilating nutrients, as well as maintaining body temperature and hormonal balance.

When pitta is balanced, it contributes to a strong appetite, good digestion, mental clarity, and effective decision-making. Imbalanced pitta, however, may lead to issues like heartburn, inflammation, excessive sweating, irritability, and anger.

How to balance pitta dosha

To bring balance to the spirited pitta dosha, consider these approaches:

- Consume foods that offer nourishment and rejuvenation, featuring sweet, bitter, or astringent flavors, such as fruits and coconut water. Gentle herbs and spices like dill, mint, and cinnamon can also prove advantageous.
- Participate in regular, non-competitive physical activities such as hiking or swimming, which also promote meditation and a connection with nature. For the industrious pitta type, striking a balance between work and personal life and engaging in self-care is essential.
- Steer clear of stimulants like caffeine, acidic foods, and items that are fermented, dense, or overly spicy.

KAPHA

Kapha dosha is the product of the water and earth elements, manifesting as heavy, slow, cool, oily, smooth, dense, soft, stable, and sticky qualities. Kapha is responsible for providing structure, strength, and stability to the body. It also ensures proper lubrication of the joints and tissues, as well as regulating the immune system.

When kapha is in balance, it supports a strong body, healthy skin, and emotional stability. An excess of kapha qualities, however, can result in weight gain, congestion, sluggishness, and feelings of attachment or resistance to change.

How to balance kapha dosha

Attaining balance in the kapha dosha with these techniques:

- Avert idleness by rising early and avoiding naps. For the kapha dosha, remaining active and engaged throughout the day is more advantageous.

- Consume meals that include warm, nourishing ingredients like quinoa and vibrant vegetables, as well as piquant spices such as cayenne and ginger. Opt for lighter proteins like chicken and turkey instead of heavier meats like beef. These choices help invigorate the metabolism and counteract the kapha's tendency toward sluggishness.

- Periodically introduce variety into your daily activities, integrating more physical and mental stimulation, including exercise and meditation. Seek methods to maintain a warm body temperature, such as spending time in a sauna or taking a walk under the sun.

The Ayurveda Cookbook for Women

Ayurvedic Approach to Nutrition and Cooking

Ayurveda is an ancient Indian system of medicine that emphasizes a holistic approach to health and wellness. In Ayurveda, nutrition and cooking are considered crucial components of maintaining a balanced mind and body. The Ayurvedic approach to nutrition and cooking involves understanding the unique needs of each individual and utilizing food as medicine to address imbalances in the body.

According to Ayurveda, there are three doshas or energies that govern our physical and mental functioning. These doshas are known as Vata, Pitta, and Kapha. Each dosha has its own set of characteristics and is associated with specific body types, personality traits, and health concerns.

In Ayurveda, food is used to balance the doshas and maintain overall health and wellness. The ideal diet for each individual depends on their dosha type, as well as their age, gender, and overall health status. For example, Vata types tend to benefit from warm, nourishing foods that are high in healthy fats and proteins, while Pitta types benefit from cooling foods that are low in fat and spice. Kapha types benefit from foods that are light and dry, as well as warm and spicy.

Cooking methods and food preparation are also important in Ayurveda. Foods should be cooked in a way that preserves their natural nutrients and flavors while also making them easy to digest. This can include methods such as steaming, baking, and roasting, as well as the use of digestive spices such as cumin, coriander, and ginger.

In addition to the specific dietary recommendations for each dosha type, there are also general principles of Ayurvedic nutrition that can benefit everyone. For example, Ayurveda emphasizes the importance of eating a main meal at lunchtime when digestion is strongest, and of eating in a calm and mindful manner, without distractions such as television or phone use.

Safety and Possible Adverse Effects of Ayurvedic Diet

The principles of an ayurvedic diet, such as eating seasonally, having a larger lunch and a smaller dinner, and avoiding late-night snacking, are generally considered safe for most healthy individuals. However, if you are taking medication that requires specific meal timing, it's recommended to consult with your doctor before making any changes to your diet.

It is crucial to be cautious when using Ayurvedic herbs and supplements without the guidance of a certified Ayurvedic practitioner. While ashwagandha is a popular ayurvedic herb that is widely available in supplement form and added to some foods and drinks, it's important not to go overboard with it. As herbs are potent, it is essential to be careful with the dosage and use them as advised.

If you are pregnant or breastfeeding, it is not recommended to take herbal supplements. It's important to discuss any supplements you may be considering taking with your doctor and consult with a certified ayurvedic practitioner or integrative doctor, or nutritionist who has knowledge of the ayurvedic diet. They can help you incorporate these supplements into your eating routine in the safest and most effective way possible.

Seasonal Eating and Eating for Your Body Type

When it comes to health and wellness, diet is a powerful tool in Ayurveda. However, many people may be left wondering: "Which diet is suitable for me?" The answer to this question is not one-size-fits-all. Each person's body type, or Dosha, responds uniquely to food. For instance, Vata individuals may have difficulty tolerating dry foods, while Kapha individuals may struggle with food that causes water retention.

It may sound complicated, but following an Ayurvedic diet is simpler than you might think. There is no need to memorize a long list of foods. Instead, Ayurveda provides basic principles for classifying foods. As each Dosha benefits from certain qualities in their food choices, the initial step is to determine your body type. First, find your Dosha.

The Seasonal Approach

In contrast to the message that modern grocery stores may convey, food changes with each season. According to Douillard, "Nature's nutritional cycle took a year to complete." Therefore, the goal is not only to consume fruits and vegetables that are in season but also to follow seasonality in your meals. Here are some general recommendations from Douillard to begin with:

SPRING	Opt for fresh leafy greens that are harvested in the spring. Dandelion tea is also recommended.
SUMMER	Eat fresh, light produce that is rich in water to balance out hydration.
FALL	Focus on nuts, seeds, and grains (to store energy for the winter), as well as end-of-summer produce.
WINTER	Consume warm soups, hearty stews, and more nuts during the colder months.

The Six Tastes

Ayurveda combines six main tastes in specific ways to create meals, as outlined in a review.

1. SWEET	Soothe and satisfy vata and pitta, but too much can cause weight gain and exacerbate kapha. Examples include honey, rice, grains, pasta, meat, dairy, and sugar.
2. SOUR	Balance vata by stimulating appetite and aiding digestion, but excess can disrupt pitta and kapha energies. Examples include vinegar, citrus, pickled foods, and berries.
3. SALTY	Balance vata by stimulating appetite and enhancing flavor, but excess can throw off pitta and kapha energies. Examples include soy sauce, fish, salt, and salted/cured meats.
4. PUNGENT	Balance kapha but excess can disrupt pitta and vata energies. They stimulate sweat glands and clear sinuses. Examples include cayenne, cloves, black pepper, ginger, chilies, mustard, onions, and garlic.
5. BITTER	Detoxify organs and balance kapha and pitta, but excess can throw off vata energies and cause digestive distress. Examples include broccoli, beets, celery, sprouts, kale, and green and yellow vegetables.
6. ASTRINGENT	Reduce inflammation and balance kapha and pitta, but too much can affect vata energies. Examples include lentils, cauliflower, pomegranates, grapes, green apples, and beans.

To ensure optimal health and well-being, Ayurveda recommends eating all six tastes at every meal to balance and satisfy your dosha energy while maximizing the intake of vitamins, nutrients, and minerals. Indian cooking embodies this principle with its diverse range of spices, pastes, and chutneys present at every meal. It's worth noting that most foods, spices, and herbs contain more than one taste. For instance, turmeric can be astringent, bitter, and sweet; oranges are sour and sweet, and apples can be astringent and sweet.

Here are the recommended tastes for each dosha to balance and satisfy their energy:

· Vata: sweet, sour, salty

· Pitta: sweet, bitter, astringent

· Kapha: pungent, bitter, astringent

Principles of Food Combination

In addition to taste, Ayurveda recommends certain food combinations that are easier to digest and support digestive fire. For instance, some foods with competing flavors can be hard on the gut, such as sour and sweet.

It is important to note that many Ayurvedic principles have not been validated by conventional nutritional research. Therefore, individuals with chronic conditions such as diabetes should consult their healthcare provider before making any dietary changes.

Here are a few general food pairing tips:

· Avoid combining fruit and dairy, such as adding berries to yogurt or milk in a fruit smoothie. Fruits break down quickly during digestion and convert into sugar, while dairy proteins take longer to digest, resulting in gas accumulation in the belly. Lower-sugar fruits like berries are better paired with nuts, seeds, and grains, as recommended by some practitioners.

· Eat most fruits, particularly melons, on their own since they are rapidly digested in the gut, according to Plumb.

· It is preferable to keep cheese, and legumes separate since they can be difficult to digest.

· Cook vegetables together as doing so can balance them out to help with digestion, according to the Ayurvedic Institute. Additionally, it is advisable to keep raw and cooked vegetables separate, as suggested by Banyan Botanicals.

Eating for Your Dosha

Ayurvedic philosophy teaches that your constitution or dominant energy type, known as your Dosha, influences what and how you should eat. The three primary doshas are Vata (air and ether elements), Pitta (fire and water elements), and Kapha (earth and water elements).

The aim of Ayurvedic eating is to balance your Dosha (s) using food. You can do this by selecting foods with opposite elemental properties to your Dosha or doshic combination. A certified Ayurvedic practitioner can help determine your individual constitution to develop a personalized Ayurvedic diet and wellness routine. Here are the basics of eating for each Dosha:

VATA DOSHA

Vata correlates to the air and ether elements, and individuals with a Vata-dominant dosha are typically cold and dry. They may experience bone and joint problems (physically) and distraction and spaciness (psychologically).

- Eat warm, moist, oily, and grounding foods such as warm soups and stews, avocados, eggs, butter, and sweet potatoes. Drink warm water.
- Avoid raw salads and bitter foods.

PITTA DOSHA

Pitta correlates to the fire and water elements, and individuals with a Pitta-dominant dosha love spicy and hot foods. They are prone to overheating and associated reactions like anger, aggression (emotionally), migraines, and rashes (physically).

- Eat cooling, watery foods such as coconut, cucumbers, zucchini, freshwater fish, rice dishes, and lentils. Calming and cooling foods can help balance Pitta. Additionally, grains, pasta, and bread that supply sugar or sweetness may soothe an aggravated Pitta's needs.
- Avoid overly spicy foods, red wine, and vodka.

KAPHA DOSHA

Kapha correlates to the earth and water elements, and Kapha-dominant individuals are nurturing and may carry extra weight. To balance their cold and wet constitution, they should consume dry foods.

- Eat grains like quinoa and millet, ghee, butter, and olive oil (in moderation to avoid excess calories), and warm spices like turmeric, cumin, coriander, black mustard seed, ginger, and cinnamon.
- Avoid heavy, cold, and wet foods like avocados.

Mind-Body Connection and Eating for Emotional Balance

The food we eat has a significant impact on our mental and emotional health. In order to achieve balance, it's important to eat foods that calm any imbalances and avoid foods that exacerbate them. To determine which foods are best, it's helpful to consider the qualities of the emotional imbalance and the qualities of the food. For example, anxiety is characterized by light, mobile, cold, and dry qualities, so it's best to avoid foods with similar qualities and instead choose foods with opposing qualities like heavy, grounding, warm, and moist. Understanding your dosha can also help in creating a diet that pacifies your particular emotional imbalance. Maintaining a consistent meal schedule and avoiding foods that cause blood sugar fluctuations are also important for emotional balance.

Anger, Short Temper, and Irritation

The Pitta dosha imbalances can manifest as anger, irritation, and a short temper. These emotions are associated with the qualities of being hot, sharp, and penetrating and may lead to excessive judgment and criticism. If you are experiencing any of these imbalances, it would be helpful to follow a Pitta-reducing diet that consists of cooling, soothing foods.

To alleviate the heat associated with anger and irritation, opt for foods with sweet, bitter, and astringent tastes. Examples of these foods include sweet and juicy fruits (such as ripe peaches, mangos, and red grapes), bitter vegetables (like kale and leafy greens), astringent fruits (such as apples and pomegranates), and astringent vegetables (like asparagus and celery). Incorporating foods like whole milk, homemade almond milk, ghee, basmati rice, rice pudding, whole wheat, oats, coconut, and avocado can also help to cool and soothe the mind. Other cooling additions to the diet include lime, cilantro, cilantro juice, coconut oil, aloe vera juice, and maple syrup. For protein sources, consider egg whites, mung dal, black-eyed peas, black beans, chickpeas, quinoa, white meat chicken (if applicable), and freshwater fish (if applicable).

It is important to avoid sharp, penetrating, and heating foods that can trigger anger and irritation. This includes spicy foods, salty foods, oily foods, fried food, chili pepper, cayenne pepper, black pepper, vinegar, fermented foods, citrus fruits (except for lime), pickles, sesame oil, inflammatory foods, red meat, pork, saltwater fish, processed foods, alcohol, tobacco, coffee, caffeine, and excessive eating out.

Maintaining a consistent and healthy meal schedule with lean protein and fiber can also help to balance emotions. Hunger and low blood sugar levels can trigger anger and irritability, so consider having a small, healthy snack between meals, such as a couple of dates, a small cup of rice pudding, or a piece of whole wheat toast with coconut oil or ghee. Take a few deep belly breaths before each meal to calm your energy and clear your mind. Avoid eating while working, arguing, or engaging in heavy conversation, as these activities can further exacerbate imbalances.

Bipolar Disorder

Since the nature of Bipolar Disorder is fluctuating, a proper and consistent meal schedule filled with lean protein and high fiber will be necessary to stabilize the energy and blood sugar levels and thus stabilize the mood. Focus on the dietary recommendations for hyperactivity and depression during the respective episodes. Always avoid refined grains, refined sugar, excessive sweets, simple carbs, processed foods, and junk food.

Depression

Depression is related to excessive Kapha dosha in the mind and a slow, sluggish digestive fire. To uplift your mood and improve your digestion, favor lightening foods like steamed veggies, bitter greens, mung dal, legumes, broth-based soups, quinoa, millet, and buckwheat. Spices like turmeric, black pepper, and cinnamon can stimulate digestion and energize the mind. Also, eat foods rich in omega-3 fatty acids, antioxidants, and B vitamins. Avoid heavy, dense, and hard-to-digest foods like dairy, wheat, gluten, refined grains, white sugar, sweets, processed foods, and fried food. Eat your largest meal midday, avoid eating after 6 pm, and never lay down after eating.

Fear, Anxiety and Worry

In today's fast-paced society, anxiety is becoming more and more common. Anxiety is a Vata-type emotional imbalance, but it can affect people of all body types. To ground the energy and calm the mind, it's essential to eat a healthy diet filled with warm, well-cooked, oily, and liquid foods. Avoid under-eating, skipping meals, and eating cold, raw, and light foods that increase the qualities related to anxiety. Also, ensure that you eat your meals sitting down in a peaceful environment with a clear mind.

Foggy, Dull Mind

A dull, foggy mind is related to excessive Kapha dosha in mind. To create clarity in mind, avoid dulling foods like dairy, wheat, gluten, white sugar, refined grains, heavy meats, and processed foods. Favor-stimulating, lightening, and sharp foods like spicy foods, bitter greens, steamed vegetables, broth-based soups, quinoa kitchari, mung dal, and legumes. Also, add heating spices like ginger, black pepper, and turmeric. To enhance digestion and mental clarity, sip on a strong ginger tea infusion between meals and take a digestive aid before each meal. Avoid snacking, grazing, and overeating, and take a brisk walk after meals.

Restless and Hyperactivity

Mind Hyperactivity and a restless mind are similar to anxiety and often occur together. A Vata-reducing diet can help to calm the airy, spacey, restless kinetic energy that characterizes hyperactivity. Favor heavy, dense, and grounding foods like whole grains, steamed veggies, root veggies, soups, stews, and lean meat. Avoid foods that increase lightness and mobility, such as refined sugar, fruit juice, dried fruit, refined grains, and caffeine. It's also essential to eat your meals at regular times and avoid eating on the go, grazing, or overeating.

Trouble Sleeping – Insomnia

If you are having trouble falling or staying asleep, it may be related to an excess of Vata dosha in the mind and body. The qualities associated with insomnia are light, mobile, and dry, and therefore a diet that is grounding, nourishing, and calming will be beneficial.

To support healthy sleep, it is important to consume foods that are rich in tryptophan, an amino acid that helps the body produce serotonin and melatonin, hormones that regulate sleep. Foods that are high in tryptophan include turkey, chicken, eggs, nuts and seeds (especially pumpkin seeds), beans, lentils, tofu, and dairy products (in moderation).

Additionally, eating foods that are high in magnesium, such as leafy green vegetables, nuts, seeds, whole grains, and legumes, can also promote relaxation and help with sleep. Other helpful foods for promoting sleep include warm, nourishing soups and stews, cooked vegetables, whole grains, warm milk with honey, and herbal teas such as chamomile and valerian root.

It is also important to avoid foods and drinks that can interfere with sleep, such as caffeine, alcohol, spicy or heavy foods, and sugary or processed foods. These foods can disrupt the natural sleep cycle and make it difficult to fall asleep or stay asleep throughout the night.

In addition to focusing on the foods you eat, it is also important to establish healthy sleep habits. This includes maintaining a consistent sleep schedule, avoiding stimulating activities before bedtime, creating a relaxing bedtime routine, and creating a peaceful sleep environment.

Embracing the Ayurvedic Lifestyle

In Chapter 2, I invite you to embrace the Ayurvedic lifestyle, a holistic approach to well-being that has stood the test of time. By adopting the principles of Ayurveda, we learn to harmonize our bodies, minds, and spirits with the natural rhythms of life. This ancient wisdom enables us to cultivate self-awareness, balance, and optimal health by focusing on our unique constitutions, daily routines, and mindful eating habits. By immersing ourselves in the Ayurvedic way of living, we can attain a sense of equilibrium and vitality, empowering us to lead more fulfilling and healthy lives. Join me on this transformative journey as we uncover the secrets of Ayurveda and learn to live in harmony with our true nature.

Ayurvedic Meal Planning and Preparation

In our fast-paced modern world, it's crucial to be organized and well-prepared to enjoy nutritious and life-giving meals. Ayurveda emphasizes the importance of consuming fresh food with high prana (life force) levels. By planning and preparing your meals mindfully, you can enjoy delicious, wholesome food without sacrificing time or budget.

Meal Plan

Meal Planning for Busy Schedules	Time constraints often hinder our ability to enjoy nourishing, home-cooked meals. By planning your meals for the week ahead, you can save time, money, and reduce food waste. Make meal planning an enjoyable weekend routine, taking into account your work schedule, social events, and your body's needs. Choose familiar meals and experiment with new recipes on slower days. Consult cookbooks and blogs for culinary inspiration.
	Create a grocery list that includes ingredients for new recipes and staple items such as cilantro, leafy greens, root vegetables, and fresh dairy. This way, you can plan your meals while still having the flexibility to mix and match fresh ingredients.
Batch Prepping for Fresh Daily Meals	Instead of batch cooking, which involves reheating large portions throughout the week, consider batch prepping. This technique allows you to cook fresh meals daily using pre-prepared ingredients. For example, wash, peel, and cut durable ingredients after grocery shopping and store them in the refrigerator. Prepare lighter, more perishable ingredients, such as greens, the night before use. You can also create pre-blended spice mixes for chai, chutneys, kitchari, or other soups and stews.
Stocking a Well-Organized Pantry	A well-stocked pantry saves time and money on grocery shopping. Ayurvedic cooking utilizes affordable, bulk ingredients that can be purchased at local markets or online. Keep your pantry stocked with whole grains, legumes, nuts, seeds, and spices suitable for your body

The Ayurveda Cookbook for Women

type and digestive capacity. Use glass jars or sealed containers for storage to keep your pantry organized and visually appealing.

Time-Saving Tools for the Ayurvedic Kitchen	The right tools can make cooking easier and more enjoyable. Modern tools like the InstantPot and VitaClay can save time in the kitchen, but traditional tools are equally effective. Choose cookware made from natural materials such as wood, clay, cast iron, and steel to avoid harmful chemicals. Essential items for a well-equipped Ayurvedic kitchen include ceramic pots, cast-iron skillets, stainless steel saucepans, pressure cookers, rice cookers, baking dishes, high-speed blenders, wooden utensils, quality knives, and glass storage containers.
Cooking for Any Size Group	When cooking for yourself or others, adjust your portions accordingly. A quarter cup of dried beans or rice is an appropriate serving size for one person, while a handful of raw vegetables or two handfuls of cooked greens should suffice. With these guidelines in mind, you can scale recipes to accommodate any number of people. By cooking separate dishes, such as whole grains, legumes, and vegetables, you can cater to the preferences of picky eaters or those who prefer meat.

Meal Preparation

In order to create Ojas, rather than Ama, and promote higher states of consciousness, it is essential to follow Ayurvedic guidelines related to food and eating. These include taking your main meal at noon, eating comfortably seated with your primary attention on your food, stopping eating when your hunger is satisfied, favoring food that is freshly prepared with love from wholesome ingredients, and cultivating a preference for a lacto-vegetarian diet.

Making Main Meal	To make lunch the main meal of the day, it is important to have a balance of all six tastes. For the average American, this means eating dinner at lunchtime and including some legumes to provide the astringent taste that is commonly missing. Investing in a wide-mouth stainless steel thermos for your entrée, a BPA-free beverage container for your lassi, and a non-reactive food storage container for your dessert can make it easier to bring your lunch to work.

Cooking Freshly Prepared with Love for One	If you are cooking for yourself, start with something simple and versatile like kichari. Allow 3-4 Tbs. of dry grain and 1.5-2 Tbs. of dried legume per person per meal. Be thoughtful in your purchases of fresh vegetables to avoid waste.
Grocery Shopping Made Easy	To prepare healthful food, you need to have suitable ingredients. Stock up on grains, legumes, nuts, seeds, dried fruits, oils, and spices, and keep a reserve of durable fruits and vegetables like apples, carrots, cabbage, and sweet potato. Look for the best value in what's available according to the season and whatever Dosha you want to balance.
Managing Different Doshas	Balance Vata and Pitta by working the common ground and going with Pitta-balancing spices. Accommodate a light diet by avoiding heavy foods for breakfast or dinner and adjusting only for lunch. If reconciling a non-vegetarian and a vegetarian, cook a vegetarian meal plus one meat dish that could be served as a soup, and offer heavier foods as a side dish or add-on option for Lacto-vegetarian or vegan meals.
Balancing Light and Heavy Foods in a Family Meal Plan	It's important to consider the lightness or heaviness of foods when adjusting meals for breakfast, lunch, and dinner. Heavy foods such as eggs, animal flesh (especially red meat and fish), soy, cheese, sour cream, yogurt, avocado, root vegetables, banana, fried food, sweet treats and nuts should be avoided during breakfast and dinner. Lunch is the ideal time to adjust for the lightness or heaviness of the foods. When cooking for both non-vegetarians and vegetarians, the simplest approach is to prepare a vegetarian meal with one meat dish that can be served as a soup at dinner or again at lunch the next day. This will provide a balanced meal for non-vegetarians and will help them consume more legumes in their diet. If everyone is lacto-vegetarian or vegan, it's easy to offer heavier foods as a side-dish such as cooked root vegetables or add-on options like roasted nuts, sour cream, or cheese. Desserts can be a happy ending to any meal, especially if made with wholesome ingredients. Those who are watching their weight can still enjoy a taster bite of dessert.

The Ayurveda Cookbook for Women

Ayurvedic Cooking Tips and Tricks

Ayurveda offers valuable cooking guidelines in addition to eating advice. These recommendations aim to help you prepare meals that are nutritious, hygienic, and delicious. Initially, I didn't pay much attention to these guidelines during my Ayurvedic journey. However, after incorporating them, I experienced significant benefits. Here are some key Ayurvedic cooking recommendations:

Thoroughly Clean Your Ingredients

You may wonder why it's necessary to clean ingredients since they'll be exposed to heat during cooking. While heat does kill germs on the surface of vegetables and fruits, it doesn't always eliminate chemicals that might be present. That's why it's essential to clean your ingredients thoroughly before cooking. Plus, it only takes a few extra minutes!

Properly Wash Your Cookware

It's no secret that clean cookware is essential for hygienic cooking. However, it's crucial to take the time to ensure your pans, vessels, and other cookware items are free from leftover food particles, which could become toxic. Spending a few extra minutes cleaning your cookware can help protect your health.

Reducing Deep-Frying

Deep-frying is a popular cooking method that adds a rich taste and crispy texture to foods. However, it's essential to minimize deep-frying in your regular meal preparation due to its potential health risks. Deep-fried foods are often high in calories, unhealthy fats, and can lose much of their nutritional value during the cooking process.

To maintain a healthier diet, consider reducing the frequency of deep-fried foods in your meals. Instead, explore alternative cooking methods such as baking, grilling, steaming, or sautéing. These techniques not only help retain more of the food's essential nutrients but also reduce the number of unhealthy fats consumed.

In situations where you prefer a fried texture, opt for shallow frying or pan-searing to use less oil. Additionally, boiling or steaming your food before frying it can also help preserve nutrients while still providing a satisfying taste.

Remember, moderation is key. It's acceptable to enjoy deep-fried foods occasionally, but it's essential to balance them with more nutritious meal options to maintain a healthy lifestyle.

Incorporating Ayurvedic Cooking into Your Daily Life

Focusing on the balance of body, mind, soul, and senses, Ayurveda is an all-encompassing approach to health and vitality. With roots in Tibetan medicine, traditional Chinese medicine, and early Greek medicine, the goal of Ayurveda is to achieve and maintain lifelong health and balance through daily, weekly, monthly, and seasonal routines.

To experience the benefits of Ayurveda, try incorporating some of its principles into your daily life, such as making lunch your largest meal, adopting daily detoxification practices, incorporating spices into your diet, exercising mindfully, and planning your day for balance and peace of mind.

By making lunch your largest meal, you can capitalize on the peak of your digestive faculties at midday. Consuming lighter meals in the morning and evening is more harmonious with your body's natural digestive processes.

Ayurveda emphasizes daily detoxification through a diet rich in whole foods, vegetables, fruits, whole grains, and beans. Drinking warm water with lemon or honey in the morning can also aid detoxification, as can using a neti pot, tongue scraper, or practicing oil pulling.

Cooking with spices is essential in Ayurvedic cuisine. Incorporating ginger, turmeric, garlic, cumin, black pepper, and other spices can not only add flavor to your meals but also provide numerous health benefits.

Ayurveda encourages mindful exercise, with a focus on lifelong health and vitality. Listening to your body and choosing appropriate exercises based on your energy levels and the seasons can help maintain balance and well-being.

Lastly, organizing your daily routine in advance can promote mental, emotional, and physical harmony. Scheduling work, family, exercise, and relaxation time ensures that you take care of yourself and the things that matter most to you. Ayurvedic practitioners recommend an early bedtime and waking schedule to make the most of the productive morning hours and restorative pre-midnight sleep.

How Ayurveda Fits into Modern Health and Wellness Trends

In recent years, modern health and wellness trends have increasingly embraced holistic and natural approaches to well-being. Ayurveda, an ancient system of medicine and lifestyle, fits seamlessly into this contemporary shift towards holistic health. Its emphasis on balancing body, mind, and spirit, along with its focus on personalized nutrition, stress management, and preventive care, aligns with the growing desire for a more integrated and sustainable approach to overall wellness. By incorporating Ayurvedic principles into our daily lives, we can enhance our physical, mental, and emotional well-being, ultimately achieving a higher quality of life in today's fast-paced world.

Health Benefits

1. Shedding Excess Weight

Ayurveda assists in your weight loss journey without using chemicals or artificial substances, all while maintaining your emotional and physical stability. Ayurvedic food contributes to detoxifying your body, purifying your skin, regulating blood flow, and reducing excess cholesterol and fat.

2. Relieving Stress

When combined with yoga practices, Ayurvedic food can help manage stress, anxiety, and even depression. There is no need to rely on pills to address these issues. Furthermore, the Ayurvedic lifestyle promotes discipline, which is highly beneficial in maintaining a balanced, stress-free life.

3. Balancing Hormones

Hormonal imbalances often underlie numerous long-term and short-term ailments, including hair loss or a lack of enthusiasm in life. Ayurveda comes to the rescue by focusing on detoxifying your body and providing essential nutrients and vitamins, ensuring hormonal balance.

4. Alleviating Inflammation

Inflammation issues often arise from inadequate sleep or an unhealthy diet. Ayurvedic food, which includes medicinal herbs like ashwagandha, turmeric, ginger, and Boswellia, not only detoxifies your body but also reduces inflammation. Boswellia is particularly effective in treating arthritis, back pain, and bowel diseases, while ashwagandha helps develop tissues.

5. Expelling Toxins

The well-known Ayurvedic treatment method, 'Panchakarma,' cleanses your body, mind, and soul by focusing on eliminating toxins from your body, which in turn supports proper body function. The Ayurvedic diet comprises various dishes and drinks that aid in detoxifying your body.

6. Reducing Disease Risk

Adhering to an Ayurvedic diet for at least 4-5 days a week can help prevent various diseases. Ayurveda works on disease prevention before they even affect your body, ensuring long-lasting health.

7. Promoting Healthy Skin and Hair

Many individuals prioritize their skin and hair health. With Ayurvedic food, there is no need for sunscreens or moisturizers, as it provides natural ingredients to keep your skin and hair healthy.

8. Combating Insomnia

At some point in their lives, everyone may experience insomnia. Ayurveda offers several remedies to prevent this issue, such as consuming warm almond milk before bed, which can significantly improve sleep quality.

9. Minimizing Bloating

Overeating or having disrupted bowel movements can lead to bloating, which is typically caused by excessive gas, resulting in pain, discomfort, and a distended abdomen. Ayurvedic food, rich in spices and roots like ginger, cardamom, and cumin, can help treat bloating and improve digestion.

The Ayurveda Cookbook for Women

Working with an Ayurvedic Practitioner

When seeking to improve your overall health and well-being, working with an Ayurvedic practitioner can provide a personalized and holistic approach to healing. Ayurvedic practitioners are trained to assess your unique needs and create an individualized treatment plan that addresses your specific health concerns. Below is written what to expect during a visit with an Ayurvedic practitioner and how their guidance can support your journey towards optimal health.

1. During your first visit with an Ayurvedic practitioner, they will spend time getting to know you, your medical history, lifestyle habits, and any specific health concerns you may have. This comprehensive assessment is crucial for understanding your unique constitution and identifying any imbalances that may be contributing to your health issues.

2. One of the key components of Ayurvedic medicine is the concept of doshas, which are the three primary energies (Vata, Pitta, and Kapha) that govern the body's functions. Your practitioner will determine your dominant dosha, as well as any imbalances, through a detailed evaluation that includes observing your physical appearance, asking questions about your habits and preferences, and assessing your pulse.

3. Based on the information gathered during the initial consultation, your Ayurvedic practitioner will create a tailored treatment plan that addresses your unique needs and health concerns. This plan may include recommendations for dietary modifications, herbal supplements, yoga and meditation practices, and other lifestyle changes, all designed to bring your body back into balance and promote overall well-being.

Regular follow-up appointments will allow your practitioner to monitor your progress, make adjustments to your treatment plan as needed, and address any new health concerns that may arise.

Depending on your specific health concerns, your Ayurvedic practitioner may recommend incorporating other healing modalities into your treatment plan. This could include acupuncture, massage, or conventional medical treatments. By collaborating with other healthcare professionals, your Ayurvedic practitioner can ensure that you receive the most comprehensive and effective care possible.

Combining Ayurveda with Other Healing Modalities

In the quest for optimal health and well-being, many individuals are exploring a variety of healing modalities to address their unique needs. Ayurveda, as a holistic system of medicine, can be effectively combined with other therapeutic approaches to create a comprehensive and individualized treatment plan. Integrating Ayurveda with other healing modalities can enhance the overall efficacy of the treatments and provide a well-rounded approach to health and wellness.

1. Massage and Bodywork

Many Ayurvedic treatments involve massage and bodywork techniques to stimulate the flow of energy and remove toxins from the body. Integrating Ayurvedic massage with other bodywork modalities, such as Swedish massage or deep tissue massage, can enhance the therapeutic benefits of both treatments and promote overall relaxation and stress relief.

2. Naturopathy:

Naturopathy, like Ayurveda, emphasizes the use of natural therapies to support the body's innate healing abilities. Combining Ayurvedic principles with naturopathic treatments, such as herbal medicine, nutritional supplements, and homeopathy, can provide a multifaceted approach to addressing health concerns and promoting overall wellness.

3. Traditional Chinese Medicine (TCM)

Both Ayurveda and TCM share similar philosophies, emphasizing the balance of energies within the body and the importance of harmony between the individual and their environment. By combining Ayurvedic principles with TCM techniques, such as acupuncture and herbal remedies, practitioners can create a customized treatment plan that addresses a wide range of health concerns and promotes overall wellness.

4. Western Medicine

Integrating Ayurvedic concepts with conventional Western medicine can offer a more comprehensive approach to healthcare. For example, Ayurveda can support the treatment of chronic conditions like diabetes or hypertension by focusing on dietary modifications, stress management, and other lifestyle changes, which complement the pharmacological treatments prescribed by Western medicine.

5. Yoga and Meditation:

Ayurveda and yoga have a shared origin in ancient India and share the goal of creating harmony between body, mind, and spirit. Incorporating yoga and meditation into an Ayurvedic treatment plan can enhance the healing process by promoting relaxation, stress reduction, and mental clarity, all of which are essential for overall well-being.

Combining Ayurveda with other healing modalities, individuals can create a personalized and holistic approach to health and wellness. This integrative approach can address a wide range of health concerns, support the body's natural healing abilities, and promote overall well-being for a healthier, more balanced life.

Embracing the Ayurvedic Lifestyle for Overall Health and Wellbeing

The Ayurvedic lifestyle offers a comprehensive approach to achieving optimal health and wellbeing by focusing on balancing the mind, body, and spirit. By incorporating the principles of Ayurveda into your daily life, you can enjoy improved physical, mental, and emotional health, as well as a greater sense of harmony and balance.

One of the foundations of Ayurveda is the belief that food is medicine, and the right diet can have a profound impact on your overall health. An Ayurvedic diet emphasizes fresh, whole foods that are appropriate for your specific dosha, or body type. This includes a wide variety of fruits, vegetables, grains, legumes, nuts, seeds, and spices, which are thought to help balance your unique constitution and promote optimal digestion, energy levels, and vitality.

An important aspect of Ayurvedic living is establishing a consistent daily routine that supports your overall wellbeing. This includes waking up early, engaging in self-care practices such as tongue scraping and oil pulling, practicing yoga and meditation, eating regular meals, and going to bed at a consistent time each night. By maintaining a consistent daily routine, you can help to regulate your body's natural rhythms and promote a greater sense of balance and stability in your life.

Physical activity is an essential component of an Ayurvedic lifestyle, as it helps to promote overall health, maintain a healthy weight, and support the proper functioning of your body's systems. Yoga, in particular, is highly recommended in Ayurveda, as it helps to cultivate flexibility, strength, balance, and inner peace. In addition to yoga, Ayurveda encourages engaging in other forms of exercise that are appropriate for your dosha, such as swimming, walking, or dancing.

Cultivating a regular meditation practice is an important part of an Ayurvedic lifestyle, as it helps to calm the mind, reduce stress, and promote emotional balance. Mindfulness, or the practice of being fully present in each moment, is also encouraged in Ayurveda, as it can help to cultivate greater awareness and a deeper connection to your body, mind, and environment.

Ayurveda recognizes that health is not merely the absence of disease but rather a state of complete physical, mental, and emotional wellbeing. As such, an Ayurvedic lifestyle emphasizes the importance of addressing the root causes of health issues and working to bring the body, mind, and spirit back into balance. This may include the use of herbal remedies, lifestyle modifications, and other holistic healing practices to support your overall wellbeing.

The Ayurveda Cookbook for Women

Building a Healthy Ayurvedic Kitchen

In Chapter 3, we embark on the journey to build a healthy Ayurvedic kitchen, which forms the foundation of our wellness journey. By understanding and incorporating essential Ayurvedic ingredients and spices, we can create delicious and nourishing meals that cater to our unique constitutions. To achieve this, we will explore various Ayurvedic cooking techniques that not only help us enhance the flavors of our dishes but also maintain the balance of our body, mind, and spirit. Additionally, equipping our kitchen with the right tools and equipment is crucial for efficient and enjoyable cooking experiences. Let's delve into the world of Ayurvedic culinary art and transform our kitchens into spaces of healing and nourishment.

Essential Ayurvedic Ingredients and Spices

Here's a chart including all the Essential Ayurvedic Ingredients and Spices:

VEGETABLES  Artichokes, Arugula, Asparagus, Beets, Broccoli, Carrots, Cauliflower, Collards, Corn, Cucumbers, Daikon radish, Endive, Fennel, Herbs (parsley, cilantro, thyme, basil, mint, dill), Kale, Leeks, Lettuce, Parsnips, Pumpkins, Radicchio, Spinach, Sprouts, Squashes, Summer squash, Swiss chard, Turnips, Zucchini

FRUITS  Apples, Bananas, Berries, Cherries, Cranberries, Dates, Figs, Grapefruit, Lemons, Mangoes, Melons, Oranges, Papayas, Pears, Peaches, Plums, Pomegranate juice, Prunes, Raisins

GRAINS  Amaranth, Barley, Brown basmati rice, Brown rice, Bulgur wheat, Buckwheat, Corn tortillas, Millet, Oats, Quinoa, Red rice, Rice noodles, Rye, White basmati rice, Wheat

BEANS  Adzuki beans, Black beans, Chickpeas, Green lentils, Mung beans (green), Mung beans (split yellow), Red lentils, Tofu (firm), White beans

FATS

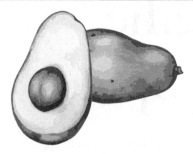

Almond meal, Avocados, Butter, Cashews, Chia seeds, Coconut, shredded, Coconut milk, Coconut oil, Cow's cheese, Cow's milk, Eggs, Flax oil, Flaxseeds, Goat cheese, Goat's milk, Hemp seeds, Olive oil, Raw nut butters, Raw nuts, Sesame oil, Sunflower butter, Sunflower seeds, Tahini, Yogurt

SPICES

Braggs Liquid Aminos, Cardamom, Chili powder, Cinnamon, Cloves, Coriander, Cumin, Fennel, Ginger, Ginger powder, Gingerroot, Mustard seeds, Paprika, Pink salt, Red chilies, dried, Sambar powder, Sea salt, Star anise, Tamari, Turmeric

EXTRAS

Apple cider vinegar, Cacao powder, Chickpea flour, Coconut sugar, Coconut water, Ginger tea, Hemp protein, Honey, Maple syrup, Molasses, Rice vinegar, Rose water, Vegetable broth

The Ayurveda Cookbook for Women

Ayurvedic Cooking Techniques

Ayurvedic cooking involves balancing the mind, body, and spirit through food. Ayurvedic cuisine aims to create harmony and promote optimal health by using specific ingredients and techniques. Here are some key Ayurvedic cooking techniques:

1. Almond Soaking	Immerse almonds in cool water for eight hours or overnight to release enzymes, making them easier to digest and more versatile in recipes.
2. Balancing Doshas	Ayurveda recognizes three doshas (Vata, Pitta, and Kapha), which are fundamental to an individual's constitution. Choose ingredients and cooking techniques that cater to your unique dosha balance, promoting harmony within your body.
3. Destemming	Remove stems from leafy greens by holding the stem in one hand and gently stripping the leaf off with the other hand. This makes the leaves easier to cook and digest.
4. Dry Roasting	Lightly roast spices in a dry pan until they release their essential oils and aromas, enhancing the dish's overall flavour.
5. Eating Seasonally	Tailor your diet to the seasons, as the body's needs change throughout the year. For instance, focus on lighter, cooling foods during summer months and heavier, warming foods during winter.
6. Freshness Matters	Whenever possible, use fresh, organic, and locally sourced ingredients to maximize nutritional value and ensure the highest quality of your dishes.

7. Grinding	Break down spices, seeds, and nuts using a mortar, pestle, or electric grinder. Freshly ground spices are an integral part of traditional Ayurvedic cooking.
8. Hand Blending	Use a hand blender to puree or mix ingredients, ensuring a smooth texture and even distribution of flavors.
9. Layering Flavors	Combine various herbs, spices, and seasonings to create a multi-layered taste profile. This technique balances the six tastes recognized in Ayurveda: sweet, sour, salty, bitter, pungent, and astringent.
10. Mindful Eating	Cultivate mindfulness while eating by chewing your food slowly, savoring each bite, and focusing on the flavors and textures. This practice can improve digestion and help you feel more satisfied with your meal.
11. Proper Food Combining	Pay attention to the compatibility of ingredients in your meals, as certain combinations can cause digestive issues or hinder nutrient absorption. For example, avoid mixing fruits with dairy or combining two different protein sources in one meal.
12. Quick Soaking	Boil grains or legumes for five minutes, then cover and let sit for one hour to achieve the same effect as overnight soaking.
13. Rinsing	Cleanse grains and legumes of impurities by rinsing them with cool water until the water runs clear.
14. Slow Cooking	Cook foods slowly over low heat to retain their nutrients and allow flavors to meld together. This method is especially useful for soups, stews, and kitchari.

The Ayurveda Cookbook for Women

15. Soaking	Reduce cooking times by soaking grains and legumes in cool water for at least one hour or overnight. Remember to adjust the cooking water in the recipe accordingly.
16. Sprouting	Soak dried foods like nuts, seeds, and beans in water, rinsing daily until they sprout. Sprouts are highly nutritious and boost digestive fire.
17. Steam Sautéing	Cook ingredients in a covered frying pan with water and no oil, allowing the natural flavors to shine through.
18. Tempering	Fry spices in oil over medium heat to release their essential oils, enhancing aroma and flavor. Tempered spices and oil are added to dishes like dals or stews.
19. Using Ghee	Ghee, or clarified butter, is a staple in Ayurvedic cooking due to its numerous health benefits. Use ghee instead of other cooking oils to enhance the taste, texture, and nutritional value of dishes.
20. Vegetable Preparation	Dice, slice, or chop vegetables ahead of time and store them in airtight glass containers for use the next day. This saves time while still allowing for fresh, home-cooked meals.

By incorporating these additional Ayurvedic cooking techniques, you can further enhance your culinary skills and create meals that nourish your body, mind, and spirit.

Kitchen Tools and Equipment

Glass Carafe Blender		A powerful blender ideal for blending hard or fibrous ingredients, such as juices and chutneys.
Food Processor		Occupies more space, but perfect for grinding nuts and preparing chunky chutneys or smooth pâtés.
Hand (Immersion) Blender		Great for blending nut milks and pureeing soups, with easy cleaning and suitable for hot soups.
Pressure Cooker		Reduces cooking time for legumes and hard vegetables, ensuring well-cooked and easily digestible beans.
Rice Cooker		An electric appliance with preset options for convenient rice or kichari preparation.

The Ayurveda Cookbook for Women

Grater		Choose a sturdy grater with small and large grating options, such as a Microplane for gingerroot.
Mortar and Pestle		A stone mortar and pestle ideal for grinding fresh spices without retaining scents like wood does.
Spice Grinder		A grinder designated for spices, seeds, and nuts, suitable for large spice mix batches.
Pepper Mill		A wooden pepper mill filled with high-quality black or multicolor peppercorns for fresh ground pepper.
Saucepan		Invest in high-quality stainless steel saucepans for soups; avoid aluminum.
Frying Pan		A ceramic nonstick frying pan is better for steam sautéing and frying compared to Teflon-coated pans.
Cast Iron Frying Pan		Ideal for slow cooking, frying, and baking due to even heat distribution and nonstick properties.

Glass Baking Dish		Useful for recipes requiring an eight- by eight-inch square dish or a nine-inch pie dish.
Fine Mesh Sieve		Essential for rinsing grains, legumes, and vegetables with smaller holes than a colander.
Baking Sheet		Stainless steel sheets for baking cookies; use parchment paper when required.
Parchment Paper		Non-stick paper suitable for lining cookie sheets during baking.
Muffin Tins		Opt for steel muffin tins with six or twelve cups, avoiding aluminum.
Muffin Cups		Paper cups for lining muffin tins when baking dense muffin batters.

CHAPTER 4

Ayurveda Recipes for Holistic Wellness and Balance

Breakfast and Brunch

1. Warm Spiced Banana Almond Oatmeal

Ingredients:

- 1 cup oats
- 1/2 tsp ground cardamom
- 3 cups cow's milk (or 1:1 ratio of water and milk)
- 1/2 tsp ground ginger
- 1/2 tsp ground cinnamon
- 1 sliced banana
- 2 tsp flaxseed
- 1 tbsp chopped almonds
- Honey, for sweetening

Directions:

1. Heat oats, milk, cardamom, cinnamon, and ginger in a small saucepan until it boils. Then, let it simmer for 4 to 5 minutes.

2. Mix in sliced banana and chopped almonds.

3. Simmer for another 4 to 5 minutes until the milk and fruit are fully absorbed.

4. Take it off the heat and sprinkle with flaxseed.

5. Optionally add honey to taste and serve.

Prep time

2 mins

Cook time

13 mins

Servings
2

2. Coconut-Sesame Oatmeal with Cherries

Ingredients:

- 3 cups almond milk
- 1 cup oats
- 1/4 cup sesame seeds
- 1/2 cup unsweetened coconut flakes
- 1 cup cherries, halved and pitted

Directions:

1. Place oats and almond milk in a small saucepan and bring to a boil.
2. Reduce heat and let it simmer for about 15 minutes until the almond milk is fully absorbed into the oats.
3. While the oatmeal cooks, dry-toast the coconut flakes and sesame seeds in a small skillet over medium heat until they turn golden brown.
4. Take off the heat.
5. When the oatmeal is done, sprinkle it with the toasted coconut, sesame seeds, and cherries, and serve.

Prep time

3 mins

Cook time

20 mins

Servings

2

3. Spiced Oatmeal with Dried Fruits and Nuts

Ingredients:

- 2 teaspoons Sliced Almonds
- 1/3 tablespoon Honey
- 1/4 teaspoon Cinnamon
- 1/4 teaspoon Cardamom
- 1/3 tablespoon Ghee
- 3 prunes, dried
- 3 apricots, dried
- 1 1/2 cups water
- Himalayan Salt pinch
- 1 Tablespoon ginger, fresh, grated
- 1/2 cup of Oats

Prep time

Overnight soaking of almonds and dried fruits

Directions:

1. In a bowl, soak sliced almonds and dried fruits in water overnight.
2. In a pot, bring water, soaked fruits, grated ginger, and salt to a rolling boil.
3. Add oats to the boiling mixture, and reduce heat to low. Stir frequently and cook for 10 minutes.
4. Remove the pot from heat, stir once more, and cover for approximately two minutes.
5. Add ghee, spices, honey, and nuts to the oatmeal and stir well. Serve hot.

Cook time

12-15 mins

Servings

1 - 2

4. Creamy Vanilla Almond Wheat with Fresh Mango

Ingredients:

- 2 cups cream of wheat
- 2 tablespoons vanilla extract
- 1½ cups almond milk
- 2 tablespoons maple syrup
- 1 tablespoon ground cinnamon
- 2 tablespoons chia seeds
- 1 mango, peeled, pitted, and diced

Directions:

1. Heat almond milk, vanilla extract, and maple syrup in a medium saucepan over medium heat until it comes to a boil.

2. Reduce the heat to low and add cream of wheat.

3. Simmer until the mixture thickens for about 2 to 3 minutes.

4. Add chia seeds, cinnamon, and mango to the mixture and serve by sprinkling it over the top.

Prep time

2 mins

Cook time

6 mins

Servings
2 - 4

5. Cinnamon-Pear Tahini Rice Puffs

Ingredients:

· 2 cups puffed rice cereal

· 2 cups almond or rice milk

· 1 tablespoon ground cinnamon

· 1 pear, peeled, cored, and sliced

· 2 tablespoons tahini

· 1 tablespoon raw honey

Prep time

Cook time

Serving

1

Directions:

1. Take a small saucepan and put it on medium heat. Pour the almond milk in it and heat it up.

2. Take a small bowl and sprinkle the cinnamon over the pear slices. Keep it aside.

3. Once the almond milk is warm, add tahini and honey to it. Stir the mixture to blend the ingredients.

4. Take a medium bowl and pour the mixture over the cereal.

5. Finally, add the cinnamon-dusted pear slices on top and relish the dish.

6. Yogurt with Hazelnut Granola

Ingredients:

· ¼ cup almond milk

· 1⅔ cups oats

· 1½ tablespoons maple syrup

· 1 tablespoon coconut, almond, or olive oil

· 1½ tablespoons flaxseed

· 1 teaspoon ground cardamom

· ¼ cup chopped hazelnuts

· 1 teaspoon ground cinnamon

· ¼ cup chopped fresh dates or figs (not dried)

· 2 cups plain yogurt

Prep time

Cook time

Servings

2 - 4

Directions:

1. Preheat the oven to 400°F.

2. In a medium mixing bowl, combine the oats, almond milk, maple syrup, flaxseed, oil, cardamom, cinnamon, hazelnuts, and dates.

3. Spread the mixture on a baking sheet and bake for 15 to 20 minutes or until golden brown.

4. Serve warm with plain yogurt.

7. Grapefruit

Ingredients:

- 1 teaspoon raw honey
- 1 fresh grapefruit
- 1/4 teaspoon ground ginger
- 1/4 teaspoon dried cardamom (optional)

Directions:

1. In a small bowl, mix the honey, ginger, and cardamom (if using).
2. Slice off the top and bottom of the grapefruit.
3. Stand the grapefruit upright on one of the flat ends and slice the peel off from top to bottom, following the curve of the fruit.
4. Slice down the membranes to remove each grapefruit slice.
5. Place the grapefruit slices in the bowl with the honey mixture and stir gently to coat.
6. Enjoy your tasty and upgraded grapefruit breakfast!

Prep time

5 mins

Cook time

0 mins

Serving
1

8. Pistachio-Infused Banana Pancakes with Spices and Molasses

Ingredients:

- ½ teaspoon ground cardamom
- 1 teaspoon baking powder
- ½ teaspoon ground cinnamon
- ½ teaspoon ground ginger
- ½ teaspoon ground nutmeg
- 2 tablespoons brown sugar
- 1 cup chopped pistachios
- 2 cups spelt flour
- 1 teaspoon vanilla extract
- 1 banana
- 2 tablespoons butter or coconut oil for cooking
- 2 cups low-fat milk
- 2 tablespoons melted butter
- Molasses, for topping

Prep time

5 mins

Cook time

10 mins

Servings
2 - 4

Directions:

1. In a small bowl, mix the baking powder, cardamom, ginger, cinnamon, nutmeg, pistachios, brown sugar, and flour.
2. In a medium bowl, mash the banana and mix in the vanilla, milk, and melted butter.
3. Add the dry ingredients to the wet and stir until well combined.
4. Heat a griddle over medium heat and melt the butter or coconut oil.
5. Ladle ⅛ to ¼ cup of the batter onto the griddle and cook until one side is brown, about 2 minutes.
6. Flip the pancake with a spatula and cook the other side for another 2 minutes or until brown.
7. Place the pancake on a plate with the spatula.
8. Repeat with the remaining batter.
9. Serve with molasses.

9. Lemon-Blueberry Corncake's with Molasses

Ingredients:

- 1 cup buttermilk or goat's milk
- 3 eggs
- Zest of 1 lemon
- 1 cup cornmeal
- ¼ teaspoon salt
- 1 cup corn flour
- ½ teaspoon baking soda
- 1½ teaspoons baking powder
- 1 cup blueberries
- 2 tablespoons brown sugar
- 2 tablespoons coconut oil
- Molasses or honey, for sweetening

Prep time

8 mins

Cook time

5 mins

Servings

2 - 4

Directions:

1. Combine the eggs and buttermilk in a small bowl and whisk.

2. In a medium bowl, mix together the cornmeal, corn flour, lemon zest, salt, baking soda, baking powder, and sugar.

3. Add the egg-buttermilk mixture to the dry ingredients and stir gently. Add the blueberries.

4. Heat coconut oil in a large skillet over medium heat. Spoon ¼-cup dollops of batter into the pan and cook until bubbles form on the batter and the side is browned, about 3 minutes.

5. Flip with a spatula and cook until the other side is browned, about 2 minutes.

6. Serve with honey or molasses.

10. Coconut-Peach Breakfast Barley Bowl

Ingredients:

- 2½ cups water
- ½ cup pearled barley
- 1 peach, pitted and sliced
- 1–2 pinches of cardamom
- 2 tsp coconut oil
- ½ cup coconut milk
- 1 tbsp coconut sugar (optional)

Prep time

5 mins

Cook time

25 mins

Servings

2

Directions:

1. To make the barley, rinse it in a fine mesh sieve and add it to a small pot with water.

2. Cook with the lid slightly ajar for about 25 minutes or until the water is absorbed and the barley is soft. Meanwhile, take a small, heavy-bottomed pan and heat the coconut oil over low heat.

3. Add peach slices and sprinkle with a pinch or two of cardamom, sautéing them until the edges turn slightly brown.

4. Once the barley is cooked, add coconut milk, optional coconut sugar, and enough water to make it blendable using an immersion hand blender or carafe blender.

5. If you use a carafe blender, make sure to leave the lid slightly ajar to allow steam to escape while blending. Blend the mixture until it becomes smooth and creamy.

6. To serve, pour the cereal into two bowls and top them with the sautéed peaches.

11. Spring Green Frittata with Herbs and Peas

Ingredients:

- 8 eggs
- ½ cup shaved Parmigiano-Reggiano cheese
- 4 cups chopped arugula
- 2 cups spring peas (can use sugar snap peas or English peas, shelled)
- ¾ cup mixed fresh herbs (basil, cilantro, oregano, thyme)
- Sea salt
- Freshly ground black pepper
- 2 tablespoons divided butter or coconut oil
- 1 diced onion
- 1 minced garlic clove
- Fresh spring peas and arugula for garnish

Prep time
3 mins

Cook time
12 mins

Servings
4 - 6

Directions:

1. Beat the eggs in a small bowl with cheese, arugula, peas, and herbs. Add salt and pepper to taste.
2. Melt 1 tablespoon of butter in a large pan over medium heat, and sauté onions and garlic for 2 minutes.
3. Pour the egg mixture into the pan and cook until it begins to set for about 5 to 8 minutes.
4. Use a spatula to lift the eggs and let the uncooked parts flow to the pan, cooking for 2 minutes.
5. Heat the remaining 1 tablespoon of butter in a smaller pan.
6. Place the smaller pan over the larger pan with the eggs and flip the eggs into the smaller pan.
7. Cook the other side for about 3 minutes until browned.
8. Add fresh peas and arugula as a garnish, if desired.

12. Asparagus & Mushroom Egg White Scramble with Cilantro

Ingredients:

- 8 eggs, whites only
- 2 tablespoons butter or coconut oil
- 1 cup chopped mushrooms
- ½ bunch asparagus, trimmed and diced
- 1 cup fresh cilantro, chopped
- Sea salt
- Freshly ground black pepper

Prep time
3 mins

Cook time
8 mins

Servings
4

Directions:

1. Heat the butter in a big skillet over medium heat, and add the diced asparagus, chopped mushrooms, and cilantro.
2. Cook the vegetables for around 2 to 3 minutes.
3. Pour in the egg whites and scramble until they are fully cooked, which should take about 4 to 5 minutes.
4. Add salt and pepper to season.

13. Buckwheat Strawberries Cereal

Ingredients:

- 2 cups water
- 1-2 teaspoons of Everyday Sweet Spice Mix
- ½ cup raw or roasted buckwheat
- ½ teaspoon vanilla extract
- 2 teaspoons coconut oil
- 1 cup chopped strawberries
- ¼ cup shredded coconut

Directions:

1. In a medium-sized saucepan, bring 2 cups of water to a boil.

2. Rinse the buckwheat in a strainer, then add it to the boiling water along with the spice mix and vanilla extract. Reduce the heat to low, cover, and simmer for 15 minutes.

3. Remove the saucepan from heat, then add the chopped strawberries and coconut oil. Fluff the mixture with a fork and cover it again. Let it stand for 5 minutes.

4. While the buckwheat is resting, toast the shredded coconut in a small frying pan over low heat, stirring constantly until it begins to brown.

5. To serve, divide the buckwheat mixture into two bowls and sprinkle the toasted coconut on top.

Hints: If you soak the buckwheat overnight, it will cook in 10 minutes. You can also soak the coconut to soften its texture and produce a creamier cereal. If you choose to do so, skip the step of toasting the coconut.

Prep time

10 mins

Cook time

20 mins

Servings

2

14. Spiced Ginger and Clove Stewed Apples

Ingredients:

- 2 or 3 apples, peeled, cored, and chopped
- 2 tablespoons almond or corn oil
- 2 tablespoons minced fresh ginger
- ½ cup rice milk
- 10 whole cloves

Directions:

1. Heat the oil in a medium saucepan over medium heat and sauté the apples for 3 to 4 minutes.
2. Cook until the apple is mushy, about 3 to 4 minutes, after adding the ginger, cloves, and milk.
3. Take out the cloves and serve.

Prep time
5 mins

Cook time
8 mins

Servings
2

15. Sunrise Delight Smoothie: Orange and Date Fusion

Ingredients:

- 2 tablespoons flaxseed
- 1 cup almond or coconut milk
- 2 cups kale
- 1 orange, peeled
- 6 dates, pitted

Directions:

1. Blend the orange, almond milk, kale, dates, and flaxseed in a blender until smooth.
2. Pour into a glass and drink up.

Prep time
5 mins

Serving
1

16. Almond-Date Energizer Elixir

Ingredients:

- ¼ cup raw almonds
- 12 pitted dates
- 2 cups skim milk
- 1 banana

Cook time

Directions:

1. Warm the milk in a small saucepan over medium heat.

2. Blend the milk, dates, banana, and almonds in a blender until smooth.

3. Pour into serving glasses and serve.

Servings

2 - 4

17. Sunflower-Ginger Pomegranate Purifier

Prep time

Ingredients:

- 1 cup pomegranate juice
- 1 apple, cored and sliced
- ½ cup sunflower seeds
- ¼ cup pomegranate seeds
- 1 (1-inch) ginger knob, peeled
- 1 teaspoon raw honey
- 1 teaspoon coconut oil
- ⅛ teaspoon ground cardamom
- ⅛ teaspoon turmeric
- ⅛ teaspoon ground cinnamon

Serving

1

Directions:

1. Blend the apple, pomegranate juice, pomegranate seeds, sunflower seeds, ginger, coconut oil, honey, turmeric, cinnamon, and cardamom together in a mixer until creamy.

2. Pour into a glass and drink up.

18. Watermelon-Mint Sunrise Booster

Ingredients:

- 1 to 2 cups ice cubes
- 3 cups watermelon, seeded and chopped
- ½ cup almond milk
- 5 or 6 mint leaves
- 2 tablespoons almond butter

Directions:

1. Blend the watermelon, mint, almond milk, almond butter, and ice cubes in a blender until smooth.

2. Pour into a glass and drink up.

Prep time

5 mins

Serving

1

19. Peachy-Strawberry Morning Bliss Shake

Ingredients:

- ½ cup rice, soy, or almond milk
- 1 peach, pitted
- ½ cup figs, pitted
- ⅛ teaspoon ground cinnamon
- 1 cup strawberries
- ⅛ teaspoon turmeric
- 1 teaspoon flaxseed
- ⅛ teaspoon ground nutmeg

Directions:

1. Warm the rice milk in a small saucepan over medium heat.

2. Blend the milk, figs, peach, strawberries, flaxseed, turmeric, nutmeg, and cinnamon in a blender until smooth.

3. Pour into a glass and drink up.

Prep time

Cook time

Serving

Appetizers and Snacks

1. Spiced Sweet Potato Bites with Tahini Drizzle

Ingredients:

- 2 large sweet potatoes, peeled and cut into 1-inch cubes
- 2 tbsp extra-virgin olive oil
- 1 tsp ground cumin
- 1/2 tsp smoked paprika
- Salt and pepper, to taste

- 1/4 cup tahini
- 2 tbsp fresh lemon juice
- 1 tbsp maple syrup
- 1 tbsp water
- Fresh parsley, for garnish

Directions:

1. Preheat your oven to 400°F (200°C). Toss the sweet potato cubes with olive oil, cumin, smoked paprika, salt, and pepper. Spread the sweet potatoes on a baking sheet in a single layer.

2. Roast the sweet potatoes for 30 minutes or until tender and lightly browned, turning halfway through.

3. To create the tahini drizzle, whisk together tahini, lemon juice, maple syrup, and water in a small bowl.

4. Arrange the roasted sweet potato bites on a serving platter, drizzle with the tahini sauce, and garnish with fresh parsley.

Prep time

15 mins

Cook time

30 mins

Servings
4

2. Crispy Chickpea Snack Mix with Indian Spices

Ingredients:

- 2 (15 oz) cans chickpeas, drained, rinsed, and patted dry
- 2 tbsp extra-virgin olive oil
- 1 tsp ground turmeric

- 1 tsp ground cumin
- 1 tsp ground coriander
- 1/2 tsp ground ginger
- Salt and pepper, to taste

Directions:

1. Preheat your oven to 400°F (200°C). Toss the chickpeas with olive oil, turmeric, cumin, coriander, ginger, salt, and pepper. Spread the chickpeas on a baking sheet in a single layer.

2. Roast the chickpeas for 40 minutes or until crispy, stirring occasionally.

3. Remove from the oven and let cool. Enjoy as a crunchy snack or add to salads and grain bowls for added texture.

Prep time

10 mins

Cook time

40 mins

Servings
4

The Ayurveda Cookbook for Women

3. Roasted Beet Hummus with Pita Chips

Ingredients:

- 3 medium beets, scrubbed and trimmed
- 1 (15 oz) can chickpeas, drained and rinsed
- 1/4 cup tahini
- 2 cloves garlic, minced
- 3 tbsp fresh lemon juice
- 3 tbsp extra-virgin olive oil
- Salt and pepper, to taste
- Pita chips, for serving

Directions:

1. Preheat your oven to 400°F (200°C). Wrap the beets individually in aluminum foil and place them on a baking sheet. Roast for 45 minutes or until tender. Remove from the oven and let cool.

2. Once the beets have cooled, peel and dice them. Place the diced beets, chickpeas, tahini, garlic, lemon juice, olive oil, salt, and pepper in a food processor. Blend until smooth and creamy.

3. Transfer the hummus to a serving bowl and serve with pita chips.

Prep time

Cook time

Servings

6

4. Spiced Carrot and Cashew Dip with Crudites

Prep time
20 mins

Servings
4

Ingredients:

- 1 cup roasted cashews, soaked for 2 hours and drained
- 1 cup grated carrots
- 1/4 cup extra-virgin olive oil
- 2 tbsp fresh lemon juice
- 1 tsp ground cumin
- 1/2 tsp ground coriander
- Salt and pepper, to taste
- Crudites (sliced cucumber, bell pepper, celery, etc.), for serving

Directions:

1. In a food processor, combine the soaked cashews, grated carrots, olive oil, lemon juice, cumin, coriander, salt, and pepper. Blend until smooth and creamy.

2. Transfer the dip to a serving bowl and serve with an assortment of crudites.

5. Baked Turmeric Sweet Potato Chips

Prep time
15 mins

Cook time
25 mins

Servings
4

Ingredients:

- 2 large sweet potatoes, scrubbed and thinly sliced
- 2 tbsp extra-virgin olive oil
- 1 tsp ground turmeric
- Salt and pepper, to taste

Directions:

1. Preheat your oven to 400°F (200°C). Toss the sweet potato slices with olive oil, turmeric, salt, and pepper. Arrange the slices on a baking sheet in a single layer.

2. Bake for 25 minutes or until crispy and lightly browned, turning halfway through. Allow the chips to cool slightly before serving.

6. Cauliflower Fritters with Cilantro Yogurt Sauce

Ingredients:

- 1 medium head cauliflower, cut into small florets
- 2 large eggs, beaten
- 1/2 cup breadcrumbs
- 1/4 cup grated Parmesan cheese
- 1/4 cup chopped fresh cilantro
- Salt and pepper, to taste
- 1 cup plain Greek yogurt
- 1/4 cup chopped fresh cilantro
- 2 tbsp fresh lemon juice
- Salt and pepper, to taste
- 2 tbsp extra-virgin olive oil

Cook time

Directions:

1. In a food processor, pulse the cauliflower florets until they resemble coarse crumbs. Transfer the cauliflower to a large mixing bowl.

2. Add the beaten eggs, breadcrumbs, Parmesan cheese, cilantro, salt, and pepper to the cauliflower. Mix well to combine.

3. Form the mixture into small patties (about 2 inches in diameter).

Serving
4

4. Heat the olive oil in a large non-stick skillet over medium heat. Cook the fritters for 4-5 minutes per side, or until golden brown and cooked through.

5. In a small bowl, whisk together the Greek yogurt, cilantro, lemon juice, salt, and pepper.

6. Serve the warm cauliflower fritters with a dollop of cilantro yogurt sauce.

7. Figgy Nut Granola Bars with Cacao Nibs

Prep time

Ingredients:

- ½ cup oat flour
- 1 teaspoon baking powder
- ½ cup wheat flour
- ½ teaspoon ground cinnamon
- ½ cup brown sugar
- ½ teaspoon ground cardamom
- ¼ teaspoon salt
- ¾ cup almond milk
- ½ teaspoon orange zest
- 3 fresh figs, chopped
- ½ cup cacao nibs
- ½ cup pistachios, chopped

Cook time

Directions:

1. 350 degrees Fahrenheit should be used for oven temperature.

2. Mix the oat flour, wheat flour, baking powder, cinnamon, cardamom, brown sugar, and salt in a medium bowl.

3. Stir in the almond milk after adding the orange zest.

4. Stir in the figs, pistachios, and cacao nibs.

5. Pour the batter into a baking dish that has been oiled, and bake for 15 to 20 minutes.

6. After cooling, slice into bars and serve.

Servings

4 - 6

8. Honeyed Apricot Chews

Ingredients:

- 2 cups oats
- ½ cup chopped pistachios
- ½ cup fresh apricots, figs, or dates, chopped
- ½ cup shredded coconut
- ½ cup almond butter
- ¼ cup, plus 2 tablespoons honey
- 2 tablespoons flaxseed
- 1 tablespoon coconut oil
- ¼ teaspoon salt

Prep time

8 mins

Cook time

18 mins

Servings

4 - 6

Directions:

1. Set the oven's temperature to 350°F.

2. Dry toast the oats for 1 to 2 minutes, or until they turn golden brown, in a small pan over medium heat.

3. Combine the oats, apricots, pistachios, coconut, and flaxseed in a large bowl.

4. Stirring continuously, bring the almond butter, honey, coconut oil, and salt to a boil in a small saucepan over medium heat for around one minute.

5. Combine the hot mixture with the oats by adding it and stirring.

6. Spread the batter onto a square baking dish and bake for 10 to 12 minutes, or until golden brown.

7. Allow to cool, slice, and serve.

9. Sesame-Maple Energy Bites

Prep time

8 mins

Cook time

20 mins

Servings

4 - 6

Ingredients:

- 2 cups oats
- ¾ cup chopped almonds
- 1 cup figs or dates, chopped
- 1 cup shredded coconut
- 2 tablespoons flaxseed

- ¾ cup whey protein
- 1 tablespoon ground nutmeg
- ½ cup almond butter
- ¼ teaspoon salt
- 3 bananas

- ¼ cup maple syrup
- 1 tablespoon vanilla extract
- ¼ cup coconut oil
- ½ cup sesame seeds
- ¼ cup water

Directions:

1. Set the oven's temperature to 350°F.

2. Combine the oats, figs, almonds, coconut, whey protein, flaxseed, nutmeg, and salt in a large bowl.

3. Mash the almond butter, bananas, vanilla, maple syrup, coconut oil, and water in a medium bowl. If the mixture looks dry, add a tablespoon or two extra water.

4. Combine the grains and wet mixture by stirring. Sesame seeds are blended in.

5. Spread the mixture into an 8-by-8-inch or 9-by-11-inch baking sheet and bake for 20 minutes, or until golden brown.

6. Serve after cooling and cutting into squares.

10. Orange-Chocolate Zucchini Bread

Ingredients:

- Coconut oil spray
- ½ teaspoon baking soda
- 2 cups oat or barley flour
- 1½ teaspoons baking powder
- 1 teaspoon ground cinnamon
- ½ teaspoon kosher salt
- 1 teaspoon ground fennel
- 1 egg
- 1 teaspoon ground cardamom
- ¾ cup brown rice syrup
- ¼ cup coconut oil
- Zest and juice of 1 orange
- 1 teaspoon vanilla extract
- 1 cup grated zucchini
- ½ cup applesauce
- 1 cup carob chips
- ½ cup sunflower seeds
- 1 apple, grated
  (or about ½ cup applesauce)

Prep time

10 mins

Cook time

20 mins

Servings

8 - 12

Directions:

1. Heat the oven to 400 °F.

2. Use the coconut oil spray to coat a muffin pan.

3. Combine the flour, baking powder, baking soda, salt, cinnamon, powdered fennel, and cardamom in a medium basin.

4. Beat the egg in a large basin. Blend in the brown rice syrup after adding it.

5. Combine the zucchini, apple, carob chips, orange juice, coconut oil, vanilla, orange zest, and sunflower seeds.

6. Fully combine the dry ingredients before adding them.

7. Place the muffin pans with the batter into the oven and bake for 20 minutes.

8. Present hot.

11. Scallion-Pumpkin Seed Savory Muffins

Ingredients:

- 1 egg
- Coconut oil spray
- 1½ teaspoons baking powder
- 2 cups oat or barley flour
- ½ teaspoon baking soda
- 2 teaspoons dried onion flakes
- ½ teaspoon kosher salt
- 2 teaspoons garlic powder

- ½ teaspoon freshly ground black pepper
- 1½ teaspoons dried dill
- cups buttermilk
- ⅓ cup chopped scallions
- ½ cup coconut oil
- ¼ cup cilantro
- 1 cup pumpkin seeds

Cook time

Servings

Directions:

1. Turn on the oven to 400°F.

2. Use the coconut oil spray to coat a muffin pan.

3. Combine the flour, baking soda, baking powder, salt, onion flakes, garlic powder, dill, and black pepper in a medium basin.

4. Combine the buttermilk, egg, and coconut oil in another medium bowl.

5. Combine the pumpkin seeds, onions, and cilantro.

6. After adding the dry ingredients, thoroughly blend them.

7. Place the muffin pans with the batter into the oven and bake for 20 minutes.

8. Serve hot.

12. Black Pepper Lemon Cakes with Poppy Seeds

Prep time

Ingredients:

- 1 cup barley flour
- 1 teaspoon baking powder
- 1 cup rolled barley oats
- ½ teaspoon freshly ground black pepper
- ¼ teaspoon salt

- ½ teaspoon ground cinnamon
- ½ cup honey or brown sugar
- ¼ cup almond or olive oil
- ¾ cup rice milk
- Zest of 1 lemon

Cook time

Directions:

1. Set the oven's temperature to 350°F.

2. Combine the barley flour, barley oats, salt, pepper, cinnamon, and baking powder in a large basin.

3. Stir in the lemon zest, rice milk, honey, and oil.

4. Place the mixture in a square baking dish and bake for 20 minutes, or until brown.

5. Slice into bars, then offer.

Servings

13. Sun-Dried Tomato Popovers with Seeds

Ingredients:

- Coconut oil spray
- 1 tablespoon baking powder
- 2 cups oat or barley flour
- ¾ teaspoon kosher or sea salt
- ½ teaspoon baking soda
- ¼ cup coconut oil
- ½ cup sun-dried tomatoes, drained of oil and finely chopped
- 1 cup almond milk
- 1 cup poppy seeds

Directions:

1. Set the oven to 375°F

2. Apply coconut spray to a baking sheet to grease it.

3. Combine the oat flour, baking powder, baking soda, and salt in a medium basin.

4. Combine the almond milk and coconut oil in a small bowl by whisking the ingredients together.

5. Add the liquid to the dry ingredients bowl and stir..

6. Add the poppy seeds and sun-dried tomatoes by stirring.

7. Spoon batter onto the baking sheet, spaced about 15 minutes apart, and bake until golden.

8. Serve hot.

Prep time

8 mins

Cook time

15 mins

Servings
4 - 6

The Ayurveda Cookbook for Women

14. Garlic and Scallion Skillet Bread

Ingredients:

- Coconut oil spray
- 1½ cups cornmeal
- 1½ cups wheat flour
- 2 teaspoons baking powder
- 1 teaspoon sea or kosher salt
- 2 tablespoons cornstarch

- ⅓ cup ghee, melted
- ½ cup cow's milk
- 1½ cups buttermilk
- 3 tablespoons chopped scallions
- 2 teaspoons minced garlic
- ½ cup fresh chives

Directions:

1. Turn on the oven to 400°F.

2. Spray coconut oil on a baking sheet to grease it.

3. Spray coconut oil on a baking sheet to grease it.

4. Combine the ghee, buttermilk, and cow's milk in another medium bowl.

5. Stir in the scallions, chives, and garlic after thoroughly incorporating the dry ingredients.

6. After distributing the mixture into the baking dish, bake for 20 minutes.

7. Slice into squares, then serve hot.

Prep time

Cook time

Servings

6

15. Corn-Free Thyme Bread

Ingredients:

- Coconut oil spray
- 1½ cups oat or brown rice flour
- 1½ teaspoons baking powder
- 1 tablespoon tapioca flour
- ¼ teaspoon sea salt
- ½ cup soy, coconut, or almond milk
- 2 tablespoons coconut or sunflower oil
- ¼ cup fresh thyme, chopped

Prep time

10 mins

Cook time

12 mins

Servings

4

Directions:

1. Turn on the oven to 400°F.
2. Use the coconut oil spray to grease a muffin pan.
3. Combine the oat flour, tapioca flour, baking soda, and salt in a medium basin.
4. Combine the coconut oil and soy milk in a larger bowl.
5. Stir in the thyme after thoroughly incorporating the dry ingredients.
6. Spoon the batter into the muffin tins and bake for 12 minutes, or until golden brown.

16. Zesty Lemon-Ginger Tea Scones

Ingredients:

- 3 cups buckwheat flour
- Coconut oil spray
- 1 tablespoon ground cinnamon
- 2 teaspoons baking powder
- ¼ cup plus 2 tablespoons brown sugar or honey
- 2 tablespoons ground ginger
- ¼ teaspoon sea or kosher salt
- Zest of 1 lemon
- 2 cups almond milk
- ¼ cup plus 2 tablespoons ghee or sunflower oil

Prep time

8 mins

Cook time

20 mins

Servings

2 - 3

Directions:

1. Set the oven's temperature to 350°F.
2. Spray some coconut oil on a baking pan and grease it.
3. Put the buckwheat flour, baking powder, brown sugar, cinnamon, salt, ginger, and lemon zest in a medium bowl.
4. Include the almond milk and ghee and mix to incorporate.
5. Spoon batter onto the baking sheet and bake for 20 minutes, or until golden brown.
6. Present hot.

17. Seed-Studded Garlic-Coriander Flatbread

Prep time

12 mins

Cook time

10 mins

Servings

4 - 6

Ingredients:

- 1 cup black sesame seeds
- 2½ cups buckwheat flour
- 1 cup white sesame seeds
- 2 teaspoons baking powder
- 1 cup plain yogurt
- 1 teaspoon sea or kosher salt
- ¼ cup minced garlic
- ½ cup rice or almond milk
- ¼ cup ground coriander
- 2 teaspoons olive or almond oil
- Ghee or coconut oil spray, for cooking
- 1 cup warm water, divided

Directions:

1. Combine the black and white sesame seeds in a small dish.

2. Combine the buckwheat flour, baking soda, and salt in a large basin.

3. Include the yogurt, rice milk, garlic, coriander, olive oil, and 1/2 cup of water. About five minutes should be spent kneading the dough, adding extra water as required to keep it from becoming too sticky or hard.

4. Divide the naan into six balls and place on a floured board to rest for five minutes.

5. Shape the balls into narrow ovals using a rolling pin.

6. Melt the ghee in a grill pan or big skillet. Cook the ovals one at a time, for 1 to 2 minutes on each side, flipping with a spatula until each side is brown.

7. Present hot.

18. Fennel Flake Flatbread with Sea Salt

Prep time

8 mins

Cook time

8 mins

Servings

8

Ingredients:

- ½ cup fennel seeds
- 4 cups wheat flour
- 2 cups warm water
- Sea salt (go lighter for pitta)
- Coconut oil spray
- Ghee, for topping

Directions:

1. Combine the wheat flour, fennel seeds, and warm water in a large bowl until a dough forms.

2. Shape the dough into 15 to 20 palm-sized, spherical balls. Roll each ball into a thin circle using a rolling pin.

3. Cook the rolled-out chapati for 1 to 2 minutes on each side, turning with a spatula, on a heated griddle over medium heat.

4. Before serving, drizzle some ghee over top and season with sea salt.

19. Curried Onion and Herb Flatbread

Ingredients:

- 4 cups buckwheat flour
- ¼ cup garlic powder
- ¼ cup curry powder (use mild for pitta)
- ¼ cup chili powder
- 1 teaspoon sea salt
- Freshly ground black pepper
- 2 cups warm water
- 1 onion, minced
- Sea salt (go lighter for pitta)
- Coconut oil spray
- Ghee to taste

Prep time

Cook time

Servings

Directions:

1. To make a dough, combine the buckwheat flour, warm water, curry powder, garlic powder, chili powder, black pepper, and sea salt in a large bowl.

2. Stir in the minced onion after adding it.

3. Shape the dough into 15 to 20 palm-sized, spherical balls. Roll each ball into a thin circle using a rolling pin.

4. Roll out the chapati and cook it on a griddle coated with coconut oil over medium heat for 1 to 2 minutes on each side, rotating with a spatula.

5. Before serving, drizzle some ghee over top and season with sea salt.

20. Fennel-Pistachio Spiced Flatbread

Ingredients:

- ¼ cup ground fennel
- 4 cups barley flour
- 1 teaspoon sea salt
- 2 tablespoons paprika
- 2 cups warm cow's milk
- Coconut oil spray
- 1 cup chopped pistachios
- Sea salt (go lighter for pitta)
- Ghee, for topping

Prep time

Cook time

Servings

Directions:

1. Combine the warm milk, sea salt, fennel, paprika, and barley flour in a large bowl until a dough forms.

2. Stir in the pistachios after adding them.

3. Shape the dough into 15 to 20 palm-sized, spherical balls. Roll each ball into a thin circle using a rolling pin.

4. Roll out the chapati and cook it on a griddle coated with coconut oil over medium heat for 1 to 2 minutes on each side, rotating with a spatula.

5. Before serving, drizzle some ghee over top and season with sea salt.

The Ayurveda Cookbook for Women

Soups and Salads

1. Kale and Avocado Salad with Creamy Tahini Dressing

Ingredients:

- 4 cups chopped kale, stems removed
- 1 large ripe avocado, diced
- 1/4 cup sunflower seeds
- 1/4 cup dried cranberries
- 1/4 cup tahini
- 2 tbsp fresh lemon juice
- 1 tbsp maple syrup
- 1 tbsp tamari or soy sauce
- 1 small garlic clove, minced
- Salt and pepper, to taste
- 3 tbsp water

Prep time

Cook time

Servings

Directions:

1. In a large mixing bowl, combine the avocado, kale, sunflower seeds, and dried cranberries.

2. To create the dressing, whisk together the lemon juice, tahini, maple syrup, tamari, minced garlic, salt, and pepper in a small bowl. Gradually add water to achieve your desired consistency.

3. Drizzle the dressing over the salad and toss until the ingredients are evenly coated. Serve immediately or let sit for 20 minutes to allow the flavors to meld.

2. Beet and Orange Salad with Walnuts and Feta

Ingredients:

- 3 medium beets, scrubbed and trimmed
- 2 large navel oranges, peeled and segmented
- 1/4 cup chopped walnuts, toasted
- 1/4 cup crumbled feta cheese
- 1/4 cup extra-virgin olive oil
- 2 tbsp red wine vinegar
- 1 tbsp honey
- Salt and pepper, to taste

Prep time

Cook time

Servings

Directions:

1. Preheat your oven to 400°F (200°C). Wrap the beets individually in aluminum foil and place them on a baking sheet. Roast for 45 minutes or until tender. Remove from the oven and let cool.

2. Once the beets have cooled, peel and slice them into thin wedges.

3. In a large bowl, combine the sliced beets, orange segments, toasted walnuts, and crumbled feta.

4. To create the dressing, whisk together the olive oil, red wine vinegar, honey, salt, and pepper in a small bowl.

5. Drizzle the dressing over the salad and gently toss to combine. Serve immediately or refrigerate for up to 2 hours to allow flavors to meld.

3. Golden Beet and Orange Salad with Fennel

Ingredients:

- 3 medium golden beets, scrubbed and trimmed
- 2 large navel oranges, peeled and segmented
- 1 small fennel bulb, thinly sliced
- 1/4 cup chopped fresh parsley
- 1/4 cup extra-virgin olive oil
- 2 tbsp fresh lemon juice
- 1 tbsp honey
- Salt and pepper, to taste

Prep time

20 mins

Cook time

40 mins

Servings
4

Directions:

1. Preheat the oven to 400°F (200°C). Wrap the golden beets individually in aluminum foil and place them on a baking sheet.
   Roast for 40 minutes or until tender. Remove from the oven and let cool.

2. Once the beets have cooled, peel and slice them into thin wedges.

3. In a large bowl, combine the sliced golden beets, orange segments, thinly sliced fennel, and chopped parsley.

4. To create the dressing, whisk together the olive oil, lemon juice, honey, salt, and pepper in a small bowl.

5. Drizzle the dressing over the salad and gently toss to combine. Serve immediately or refrigerate for up to 2 hours to allow flavors to meld.

4. Turmeric Chickpea Salad with Mint-Yogurt Dressing

Ingredients:

- 1 (15 oz) can chickpeas, drained and rinsed
- 1/2 cup diced cucumber
- 1/2 cup diced bell pepper (any color)
- 1/4 cup diced red onion
- 1/4 cup chopped fresh mint
- 1 tsp ground turmeric
- 1 cup plain Greek yogurt
- 2 tbsp fresh lemon juice
- 1 tbsp honey
- Salt and pepper, to taste

Prep time

20 mins

Cook time

0 mins

Servings
4

Directions:

1. In a large bowl, combine the chickpeas, cucumber, bell pepper, red onion, fresh mint, and turmeric.

2. To create the dressing, whisk together the Greek yogurt, lemon juice, honey, salt, and pepper in a small bowl.

3. Pour the dressing over the salad and mix well to combine. Serve immediately or refrigerate for at least 1 hour to allow flavors to meld.

5. Spiced Cauliflower Salad with Pomegranate and Pistachios

Ingredients:

- 1 medium head cauliflower, cut into small florets
- 1 tbsp extra-virgin olive oil
- 1 tsp ground cumin
- 1 tsp ground coriander
- 1/2 tsp ground cinnamon
- 1/4 tsp ground cardamom
- Salt and pepper, to taste
- 1/2 cup pomegranate seeds
- 1/4 cup shelled pistachios, roughly chopped
- 1/4 cup chopped fresh cilantro
- 2 tbsp fresh lemon juice
- 1 tbsp honey
- 1 tbsp extra-virgin olive oil

Prep time

Cook time

Servings

4

Directions:

1. Preheat your oven to 425°F (220°C). Toss the cauliflower florets with 1 tbsp olive oil, cumin, coriander, cinnamon, cardamom, salt, and pepper. Spread the cauliflower on a baking sheet and roast for 25 minutes or until tender and lightly browned.

2. Remove the cauliflower from the oven and let it cool slightly.

3. In a large bowl, combine the roasted cauliflower, pomegranate seeds, chopped pistachios, and fresh cilantro.

4. To create the dressing, whisk together the lemon juice, honey, and 1 tbsp olive oil in a small bowl.

5. Drizzle the dressing over the salad and gently toss to combine. Serve warm or at room temperature.

6. Basil and Scallion Asparagus Bisque

Ingredients:

- 2 tablespoons coconut oil
- 2 tablespoons oat or wheat flour
- ½ cup chopped leeks (white parts only)
- ½ teaspoon ground nutmeg
- 1 bunch asparagus, trimmed and chopped
- 3 cups vegetable broth, warmed
- Plain yogurt, for garnish (optional)
- ½ cup parsnips, peeled and chopped
- ½ cup tightly packed fresh basil leaves, chopped
- 1 cup cow's milk, warm
- ½ cup chopped scallions (white parts only)
- Pinch salt

Prep time

10 mins

Cook time

20 mins

Servings
2

Directions:

1. In a large soup pot over low heat, warm the coconut oil, then sauté the leeks for approximately two minutes, or until tender.

2. Stir in the flour and nutmeg, cooking for a further 2 minutes.

3. Add the veggie broth while whisking slowly.

4. Add the parsnips and asparagus in step 4. Bring the mixture to a boil over medium heat.

5. Covered, simmer for 15 minutes.

6. Add the milk, basil, and scallions to the soup in a blender. Smooth after puréeing.

7. Add a sprinkle of salt, a few pieces of sliced asparagus, and a dollop of plain yogurt, if using.

7. Minty Vegetable and Bean Stew

Ingredients:

- 4 tablespoons coconut oil or ghee
- 2 tablespoons ground cumin
- 1 large onion, chopped
- 1 cup chopped cauliflower
- 2 tablespoons ground coriander
- 2 tomatoes, chopped
- 1 cup chopped asparagus
- 1 cup chopped cabbage
- 1 cup chopped mushrooms
- 1 teaspoon sea or kosher salt
- 1 cup chopped greens
- 4 cups vegetable broth
- 2 (14.5-ounce) cans kidney beans, drained
- 1 large handful fresh mint, chopped

Prep time

10 mins

Cook time

20 mins

Servings
6 - 8

Directions:

1. Heat the oil in a big saucepan over medium heat. For two to three minutes, add and sauté the onions.

2. Stir in the cumin and coriander before adding it to the onions.

3. Include the tomatoes, beans, greens, cauliflower, cabbage, asparagus, mushrooms, and broth. For 15 minutes, cook.

4. Sprinkle salt and mint over top before serving.

8. Lentil and Ginger Pumpkin Chowder

Ingredients:

- 2 tablespoons coconut or olive oil
- 3 tablespoons minced fresh ginger
- 1 small onion, chopped
- 4 garlic cloves, peeled and minced
- 1 teaspoon ground cumin
- 1 teaspoon turmeric
- 1 teaspoon ground coriander
- 1 teaspoon garam masala
- 1 bay leaf
- 1 (15-ounce) can pumpkin purée
- 1 cup lentils, any variety
- 6 cups vegetable broth

Prep time

5 mins

Cook time

25 mins

Servings

4 - 6

Directions:

1. Heat the coconut oil, onion, and garlic in a big saucepan over medium-high heat. Cook for 4 minutes or until browned.
2. Stir to coat the onions and garlic with the ginger, cumin, coriander, garam masala, turmeric, and bay leaf.
3. Include the pumpkin, lentils, and broth.
4. Boost the heat to its highest setting and bring the soup to a boil.
5. Reduce the heat to medium-low, then simmer for 20 minutes.
6. Take off the bay leaf before serving.

9. Toasted Almond and Curry Carrot Purée

Ingredients:

- 2 tablespoons olive oil
- 1½ pounds carrots, peeled and chopped
- 2 onions, peeled and chopped
- 1 celery stalk, chopped
- 2 tablespoons curry powder
- 6 cups vegetable broth
- 1 cup chopped toasted almonds
- Freshly ground black pepper

Directions:

1. Heat the oil in a big soup pot, then add the carrots, celery, onions, and curry powder. Cook for five minutes.

2. Add the stock and cook for 15 to 20 minutes, stirring occasionally.

3. Transfer the soup to a blender, then purée it until smooth.

4. Add black pepper and the chopped almonds to your serving.

Prep time

5 mins

Cook time

25 mins

Servings
2 - 4

10. Bean and Quinoa Artichoke Velouté

Ingredients:

- 3 tablespoons coconut oil
- ½ cup chopped celery
- 1 cup chopped onion
- 6 cups vegetable broth
- ½ teaspoon sea or kosher salt
- 3 garlic cloves, minced
- 2 (15-ounce) cans artichoke hearts, drained
- 1 cup quinoa
- 3 (15-ounce) cans chickpeas or mung beans (or 1½ cans each)
- 2 teaspoons chopped fresh rosemary
- 1 teaspoon freshly ground black pepper
- 1 tablespoon red wine vinegar (vatas can use more)

Prep time

5 mins

Cook time

23 mins

Servings
4 - 6

Directions:

1. Heat the oil in a big soup pot over medium-high heat. Add the salt, celery, garlic, and onion. For 2 to 3 minutes, cook.

2. The veggie broth should be added and boiled. Simmer for ten minutes on low heat.

3. Include the quinoa, beans, and artichoke hearts.

4. Continue to cook for 10 more minutes.

5. Add the rosemary, vinegar, and black pepper, then serve.

The Ayurveda Cookbook for Women

11. Lemony Chickpea and Spinach Consommé

Ingredients:

- ½ cup chopped onion
- 3 tablespoons coconut oil
- ½ teaspoon sea or kosher salt
- ½ cup chopped celery
- 1 teaspoon ground cumin
- 1 teaspoon mustard seeds
- 1 teaspoon ground cardamom
- 2 tablespoons minced fresh ginger
- 6 cups vegetable broth

- 3 garlic cloves, minced
- 3 (15-ounce) cans chickpeas or mung beans (or 1½ cans each)
- 3 cups spinach
- Zest of 1 lemon
- 1 teaspoon freshly ground black pepper
- 2 teaspoons fresh thyme
- 2 teaspoons chopped fresh rosemary

Directions:

1. Heat the oil in a big soup pot over medium-high heat. Add the mustard salt, seeds, cumin, cardamom, onion, and celery. Add the ginger and garlic once the mustard seeds have popped, which should take 2 to 3 minutes.

2. Prepare for two minutes.

3. Add the veggie broth and heat through.

4. Lower the heat, then simmer the food for 10 minutes.

5. After cooking for an additional 10 minutes, add the chickpeas.

6. Add the spinach, black pepper, rosemary, and thyme after stirring in the lemon zest.

12. Adzuki and Brussels Sprouts Miso Bouillabaisse

Ingredients:

- 6 cups vegetable broth
- 1 leek, chopped (white parts only)
- 2 cups Brussels sprouts, halved
- 1 cup chopped broccoli
- 2 tablespoons miso dissolved in 1

tablespoon water
- 2 (15-ounce) cans adzuki beans, drained
- ¼ cup fresh dill, chopped
- Sea salt

Directions:

1. Bring the broth to a boil in a big soup pot.

2. Lower the heat to a simmer and stir in the beans, broccoli, leek, and Brussels sprouts.

3. Prepare the food for 5–7 minutes.

4. After taking the pan off the heat, whisk in the miso and dill. Serve after adding salt to taste.

13. Coconut Chickpea and Squash Ragout

Ingredients:

- 1½ tablespoons coconut oil
- 4 garlic cloves, minced
- 1 onion, peeled and chopped (halve for pittas)
- 2 tablespoons minced fresh ginger
- 1½ cups mung beans (canned or split dried for quicker cooking time)
- 6 cups vegetable broth
- 2 cups cubed butternut squash (can use prepackaged)
- 2 (15-ounce) cans chickpeas, drained
- 2 carrots, chopped (can use prechopped)
- 1 tablespoon turmeric
- 1 (15-ounce) can coconut milk
- 1 tablespoon garam masala
- Sea salt

Prep time

5 mins

Cook time

25 mins

Servings
6

Directions:

1. Heat the coconut oil in a big soup pot over medium heat. Sauté the ginger, onion, and garlic for 3 to 4 minutes after adding them.

2. Include the veggie broth and bring to a boil. Add the mung beans, squash, carrots, chickpeas, turmeric, and garam masala after turning down the heat to a simmer.

3. For 20 minutes, simmer.

4. Include the coconut milk and stir to fully reheat.

5. Add sea salt to the dish and serve.

14. Fava Bean and Polenta Cassoulet

Prep time
5 mins

Cook time
25 mins

Servings
6 – 8

Ingredients:

- ¼ cup olive oil
- 2 (15-ounce) cans fava beans, drained
- 1 tablespoon mustard seeds
- 1 tablespoon hot curry powder
- 1 tablespoon minced fresh ginger
- 1 tablespoon ground coriander
- 1 tablespoon ground cumin
- 1 tablespoon turmeric
- 1 tablespoon ground dried thyme
- 4 garlic cloves, minced
- 1 onion, chopped
- 1 carrot, peeled and sliced (or preshredded packaged)
- 1½ cups polenta
- 8 cups vegetable broth
- 1 bunch kale, stemmed and chopped
- Lime or lemon wedges, for garnish

Directions:

1. Warm the olive oil in a large soup pot over medium heat. In approximately 2 minutes, add the mustard seeds and heat them until they pop.

2. After cooking for 2 minutes, add the ginger.

3. Include the curry powder, coriander, cumin, turmeric, and thyme. Cook for 2 minutes, or until aromatic.

4. Add the spices and toss in the onion, garlic, and carrot. For 3 to 5 minutes, cook.

5. Add the veggie broth and bring to a boil over high heat.

6. Include the polenta, reduce the heat, and let it simmer for 10 minutes.

7. Include the fava beans and kale, and simmer for an additional 5 minutes.

8. Present with slices of lime or lemon.

15. Toasted Coconut and Mint Eggplant Goulash

Ingredients:

- 1½ cups cauliflower
- 3 tablespoons ghee
- 1 large onion, diced
- 2 tablespoons turmeric
- 2 tablespoons ground cumin
- 2 teaspoons ground coriander
- 1 tablespoon paprika
- 2 teaspoons black mustard seeds
- 3 eggplants, peeled and chopped
- 3 large potatoes, chopped
- 2 tomatoes, diced
- 1 handful mint, chopped
- 1 (15-ounce) can vegetable broth
- 1½ cups unsweetened coconut flakes
- Sea salt

Prep time
5 mins

Cook time
22 mins

Servings
6

Directions:

1. Heat the ghee and add the cumin, onion, turmeric, coriander, mustard seeds, and paprika to a large soup pot over medium heat. For 2 to 3 minutes, cook.

2. Include the potatoes and eggplant and simmer for 5 minutes.

3. Cook for 15 to 20 minutes after adding the cauliflower, tomatoes, and vegetable broth.

4. Dry toast the coconut flakes for 1 to 2 minutes, or until they start to brown, in a small pan over medium heat.

5. Add the coconut, sea salt, and mint as garnish before serving.

16. Cauliflower and Lentil Hearty Stew

Ingredients:

- 8 cups vegetable broth
- 3 tablespoons olive oil
- 1 tablespoon ground coriander
- 1½ tablespoons ground cumin
- 1 tablespoon ground fennel
- 1 tablespoon turmeric
- 12 cardamom pods
- 4 bay leaves
- 4 cinnamon sticks
- 2 cups chopped cauliflower
- ¼ cup unsweetened coconut flakes
- 2 cups canned or fresh lentils
- 2 tablespoons minced fresh ginger
- 1¼ cups quinoa

Prep time
3 mins

Cook time
16 mins

Servings

6 - 8

Directions:

1. Heat the olive oil in a large soup pot over medium heat, then add the turmeric, cumin, coriander, and fennel.

2. Add the vegetable broth, coconut, cinnamon, ginger, and bay leaves and bring to a boil.

3. Reduce the heat, then stir in the cauliflower, quinoa, and lentils.

4. Simmer for ten to fifteen minutes.

5. Dish out after removing the bay leaves.

17. Tofu and Tomato Indian Masala

Ingredients:

- 4 cups spinach leaves
- 2 tablespoons coconut oil
- 3 tablespoons ground cumin
- 3 tablespoons ground ginger
- 3 tablespoons ground coriander
- 1 onion, chopped
- 1 tablespoon turmeric
- 2 (14-ounce) packages firm tofu, drained and cubed
- 1 (15-ounce) can coconut milk
- 2 (15-ounce) cans crushed tomatoes
- 1 teaspoon salt
- Orange zest, for garnish (optional)
- 1 bunch fresh cilantro leaves, chopped

Prep time

5 mins

Cook time

25 mins

Servings

6 – 8

Directions:

1. Heat the oil in a big soup pot over medium heat, then add the turmeric, ginger, cumin, and coriander.

2. Add the onion and tofu after cooking for 1 to 2 minutes.

3. Cook for 10 minutes while stirring to incorporate the seasonings.

4. Include the spinach and tomatoes and bring to a boil.

5. Reduce the heat and stir in the salt and coconut milk.

6. Simmer for ten to fifteen minutes.

7. If using, garnish with cilantro and orange zest before serving.

18. Chili and Black Rice Miso Porridge

Ingredients:

- 6 cups vegetable broth
- 1 (15-ounce) can split peas, drained
- 2 cups quick-cooking black rice
- 1 to 2 cups vata vegetables, like mushrooms, spinach, sprouts, or snow peas (optional)
- 3 tablespoons ghee
- 1 teaspoon sea or kosher salt
- 3 tablespoons cumin seeds
- 4 cardamom pods
- ¼ cup miso
- 3 tablespoons mustard seeds
- 2 tablespoons turmeric
- 4 garlic cloves, minced or chopped
- 2 tablespoons minced or chopped fresh ginger
- 2 Thai green chilies or 1 teaspoon red chili flakes (optional)
- Squeeze of 1 lemon

Prep time

5 mins

Cook time

25 mins

Servings

6 – 8

Directions:

1. Over medium heat, bring the rice and vegetable broth to a boil in a large pot.

2. Reduce the heat, then stir in the salt, veggies, and peas. Spend 15 minutes simmering.

3. Heat the ghee in a small pan over medium heat, then add the turmeric, cardamom, mustard seeds, and cumin.

4. Cook the mustard seeds for 1 to 2 minutes, or until they begin to pop.

5. Include the chiles, ginger, and garlic. Cook for two minutes while stirring to incorporate the spices.

6. Combine the rice and pea combination with the ghee mixture and miso. Garnish with a squeeze of lemon and serve.

19. Caramelized Onion Quinoa Kitchari

Ingredients:

- 3 tablespoons sunflower oil
- 3 tablespoons mustard seeds
- 3 tablespoons cumin seeds
- 4 cardamom pods
- 2 tablespoons turmeric
- 2 Thai green chilies or 1 teaspoon red chili flakes (optional)
- 2 red onions, sliced
- 2 tablespoons minced or chopped fresh ginger
- 4 garlic cloves, minced or chopped
- 1 teaspoon sea or kosher salt
- 6 cups vegetable broth
- 1 cup quinoa
- 2 (15-ounce) cans lentils, drained
- 1 to 2 cups kapha vegetables (optional)
- Squeeze of 1 lemon

Prep time

4 mins

Cook time

24 mins

Servings

6

Directions:

1. Heat the oil in a big soup pot over medium heat, then add the turmeric, cardamom, mustard seeds, and cumin. The mustard seeds should explode after 1 to 2 minutes of cooking.

2. Include the onions, ginger, garlic, and, if using, the chilies. Cook for 8 to 10 minutes while stirring to incorporate the spices.

3. Include the veggie broth and bring the mixture to a boil.

4. Increase the heat before adding the quinoa.

5. Include the lentils, salt, and any other veggies.

6. For 15 minutes, simmer.

7. Add some lemon juice as a garnish before serving.

20. Brown Rice Swiss Chard Pilaf

Ingredients:

- ¼ cup cumin seeds
- 3 tablespoons sunflower oil
- 2 tablespoons turmeric
- ¼ cup fennel seeds
- ¼ cup minced or chopped fresh ginger
- 1 cup quick-cooking brown rice

- 6 cups vegetable broth
- 1 bunch chard, stemmed and chopped
- 1 bunch fresh cilantro, chopped
- 1 to 2 cups kapha vegetables, like eggplant, onions, cauliflower, or potatoes (optional)
- Squeeze of 1 lime, for garnish

Prep time

4 mins

Cook time

18 mins

Servings

6 - 8

Directions:

1. Heat the oil in a large soup pot over medium heat before adding the turmeric, fennel, and cumin.
2. Prepare for one to two minutes.
3. After cooking for another minute, add the ginger.
4. Add the rice and turn down the heat after bringing the vegetable broth to a boil.
5. Include the veggies and chard, if using, and boil for 15 minutes.
6. Add cilantro and lime juice as a garnish before serving.

21. Sesame Seaweed Kitchari Bowl

Ingredients:

- 6 cups vegetable broth
- 3 tablespoons olive oil or ghee
- 2 tablespoons turmeric
- ¼ cup cumin seeds
- 2 tablespoons minced or chopped fresh ginger

- 2 (15-ounce) cans mung beans, drained
- 1 cup quick-cooking brown rice
- 1 bunch fresh cilantro, chopped
- 1 cup seaweed (kombu)
- 1 to 2 cups pitta vegetables (optional)
- ¼ cup toasted black sesame seeds

Prep time

4 mins

Cook time

18 mins

Servings
6

Directions:

1. Heat the oil in a big soup pot over medium heat, then add the cumin and turmeric.
2. Prepare for one to two minutes.
3. After cooking for another minute, add the ginger.
4. Include the veggie broth and bring the mixture to a boil.
5. Stir in the rice and turn the heat down.
6. Include the veggies, seaweed, and mung beans. Simmer for 15 minutes.
7. Add the cilantro and sesame seeds as a garnish before serving.

22. Tahini Drizzled Vegetable Kitchari

Ingredients:

- 6 cups vegetable broth
- 2 tablespoons ghee
- 1 tablespoon turmeric
- 1 tablespoon cumin seeds
- 1 tablespoon ground coriander
- 1 tablespoon ground cinnamon
- 1 tablespoon freshly ground black pepper
- 1 tablespoon ground cumin
- ½ tablespoon ground cloves
- ½ tablespoon sea salt
- 3 bay leaves
- 4 garlic cloves, minced
- 2 tablespoons minced fresh ginger
- 1 onion, diced
- 1 (15-ounce) can mung beans (or ½ cup dried split mung beans)
- 1 cup basmati rice
- 1 cup chopped green beans
- ½ cup shredded carrots
- 1 cup chopped asparagus
- ½ cup shelled peas
- 1 cup squash, cubed (can use prepackaged)
- 1 cup spinach
- Tahini, for drizzling

Prep time

6 mins

Cook time

19 mins

Servings

4 - 6

Directions:

1. Heat the ghee and cumin seeds in a large soup pot over medium heat.

2. Prepare for one minute.

3. Add the onion, ginger, garlic, cloves, turmeric, coriander, black pepper, cinnamon, cumin, sea salt, and other spices. For 2 to 3 minutes, cook.

4. Include the broth, rice, green beans, asparagus, carrots, peas, mung beans, spinach, and squash.

5. Bring to a boil.

6. Lower the heat, then simmer the food for 15 minutes.

7. Take out the bay leaves and serve the food with tahini on the side.

23. Spiced Tofu and Red Rice Kitchari

Ingredients:

- 2 cups leftover red rice (or quinoa if you have no leftover rice)
- 2 tablespoons coconut oil
- 3 tablespoons ground cumin
- 3 tablespoons ground ginger
- 3 tablespoons black mustard seeds
- 1 tablespoon fenugreek seeds
- 1 tablespoon fennel seeds
- 1 tablespoon ground coriander
- 1 onion, chopped
- 1 tablespoon turmeric
- 2 (14-ounce) packages firm tofu, drained and cubed
- 6 cups vegetable broth
- 1 teaspoon salt
- 4 cups spinach leaves
- 1 bunch fresh cilantro leaves, chopped

Prep time

5 mins

Cook time

19 mins

Servings

6 - 8

Directions:

1. Heat the oil in a big soup pot over medium heat, then add the turmeric, ginger, cumin, black mustard seeds, fennel seeds, and fenugreek seeds. For one to two minutes, cook.

2. Add the onion and tofu, then whisk them into the spice mixture. For 8 to 10 minutes, cook.

3. Stir in the broth and rice, and then bring to a boil.

4. Reduce the heat, simmer for 10 to 15 minutes, then serve.

5. Add salt and the spinach leaves.

6. Add cilantro as a garnish and serve.

The Ayurveda Cookbook for Women

Main Courses

1. Lemon-Zested Spiced Asparagus Spears

Ingredients:

- 1 tablespoon curry powder
- 2 tablespoons ghee or coconut oil
- 1 bunch asparagus, trimmed
- ½ teaspoon sea or kosher salt
- 1 tablespoon freshly squeezed lemon juice
- Zest of 1 lemon

Directions:

1. Ghee should be heated in a pan over medium heat.
2. Stir in the curry powder and heat for 1–2 minutes, or until you can smell it.
3. Add the asparagus and lemon juice, and simmer for 3 minutes, or until the asparagus is crisp-tender.
4. Add the lemon zest and sea salt as a garnish before serving.

Prep time

5 mins

Cook time

8 mins

Servings

2 - 4

2. Parmesan-Topped Spaghetti

Ingredients:

- 2 ounces shaved Parmesan cheese
- 4 to 6 ounces dried whole-wheat spaghetti
- 4 garlic cloves, minced
- ¼ cup olive oil
- 1 onion, sliced
- ½ cup chopped toasted walnuts
- Squeeze of 1 lemon
- Freshly ground black pepper
- Sea salt

Directions:

1. Cook the spaghetti as directed on the box in a big saucepan of boiling water.
2. After draining the pasta, save 1 cup of the cooking water.
3. Heat the olive oil in a big pan over medium heat, then sauté the garlic for a minute.
4. Include the onion and simmer for 15 minutes, or until browned.
5. Add the drained pasta to the onion mixture in the pan. Add some pasta water if you think you need a bit more "sauce."
6. Finish the dish by adding the Parmesan, lemon, sea salt, and pepper.

Prep time

5 mins

Cook time

20 mins

Servings

2

3. Cilantro and Pepper Stir-Fried Okra

Ingredients:

- 2 to 3 Thai red chilies, deseeded
- 2 tablespoons ghee or coconut oil
- 1 pound okra, sliced
- 2 tablespoons cumin seeds
- 1 tablespoon turmeric
- ½ teaspoon sea or kosher salt
- ¾ cup cilantro
- Squeeze of lemon, for garnish

Directions:

1. Ghee should be heated in a large pan over medium heat. seed cumin is added. Cook until they pop, 1 to 2 minutes.
2. Include the tomatoes and red chili. 4 to 5 minutes of cooking.
3. Add the okra and turmeric, and simmer for 3 minutes, or until the okra is cooked but still somewhat crunchy.
4. Add the sea salt, cilantro, and lemon as garnishes before serving.

Prep time

4 mins

Cook time

5 mins

Servings

2 - 4

4. French Bean and Herbed Spaghetti

Ingredients:

- 4 cups French green beans, trimmed and halved
- 4 to 6 ounces dried whole-wheat spaghetti
- 2 shallots, minced
- ¼ cup olive oil
- 2 garlic cloves, minced

- 1 cup chopped fresh parsley
- 1 cup chopped fresh basil
- 1 cup chopped fresh mint
- Squeeze of 1 lemon
- 1 cup chopped fresh cilantro
- ½ cup chopped toasted walnuts

Cook time

Directions:

1. Prepare the spaghetti as directed on the box in a big saucepan of boiling water.

2. After draining the pasta, save 1 cup of the cooking water.

3. Heat the olive oil in a big pan over medium heat, then sauté the shallots and garlic for a minute.

4. Include the beans and simmer for 3 to 4 minutes, or until they are al dente.

5. Add the drained pasta to the bean mixture in the pan. Add some pasta water if you think you need a bit more "sauce."

6. Add the lemon, walnuts, mint, cilantro, basil, and parsley before serving.

Servings
2 - 4

5. Pickled Beet and Avocado Salad with Feta

Prep time

Ingredients:

- 1 (16-ounce) jar pickled beets, quartered
- Squeeze of 1 lemon
- 1 avocado, peeled, pitted, and diced
- ½ cup crumbled feta cheese

Servings
2

Directions:

1. Divide the pickled beet quarters evenly between two serving dishes.

2. Add the diced avocado on top of the beets in each dish.

3. Squeeze the juice of 1 lemon over the avocado and beets in each dish.

4. Sprinkle the crumbled feta cheese evenly over each serving.

5. Serve the salad immediately, while the beets and avocado are still fresh and vibrant. Enjoy!

6. Pomegranate-Arugula Twist Spaghetti

Ingredients:

- 6 cups arugula
- ¼ cup olive oil
- 16 ounces dried whole-wheat spaghetti
- 3 garlic cloves, minced
- Sea salt
- 2 tablespoons pomegranate molasses
- Freshly ground black pepper

Directions:

1. Put the arugula in a big basin.
2. Prepare the pasta in a big saucepan as directed on the package.
3. Heat the oil in a small pan over medium heat. Cook the garlic for 2 to 3 minutes after adding it.
4. Include and fully heat the pomegranate molasses.
5. When the pasta is al dente, drain it while saving 1 cup of the cooking water.
6. Toss the pasta and arugula together after adding the heated oil.
7. If the pasta is too dry, add a little pasta water.
8. Add salt and pepper to taste and serve.

Prep time

3 mins

Cook time

20 mins

Servings
2 - 4

7. Garlic and Currant-Dressed Dinosaur Kale

Ingredients:

- 2 garlic cloves, sliced thin
- 2 tablespoons ghee or coconut oil
- Squeeze of 1 lemon
- 1 bunch kale, stemmed and chopped
- ¾ cup currants
- Sea salt to taste

Directions:

1. Melt the ghee and garlic in a big pan over medium heat.
2. Cook for two to three minutes.
3. Add the kale and currants, and simmer for 5 minutes, or until the kale is wilted.
4. Add salt and lemon to taste and serve.

Prep time

3 mins

Cook time

7 mins

Servings
2

8. Sesame-Asparagus Asian Noodle Stir-Fry

Prep time

5 mins

Cook time

20 mins

Servings

2 - 4

Ingredients:

- ¼ cup sesame oil
- 2 garlic cloves, minced
- 4 to 6 ounces dried whole-soba, udon, or rice noodles
- 4 cups chopped asparagus
- ¼ teaspoon red chili flakes
- ¼ cup soy sauce
- ½ cup chopped fresh cilantro
- ¼ cup raw honey
- ½ cup chopped fresh basil
- ½ cup toasted sesame seeds
- ½ cup chopped toasted peanuts

Directions:

1. Cook the pasta as directed on the box in a big saucepan of boiling water. Drain.
2. Heat the sesame oil in a large pan over medium heat. For two minutes, sauté the garlic and chili flakes.
3. Add the asparagus and simmer for 3 to 4 minutes, or until al dente.
4. Include the basil, honey, cilantro, and soy sauce.
5. Toss the drained pasta with the oil and spice mixture in the skillet.
6. Sprinkle the sesame seeds and peanuts on top before serving.

9. Minty Asian Fennel Slaw

Prep time

5 mins

Servings

2

Ingredients:

- ½ cup chopped cabbage (can use prepackaged)
- 1 large fennel bulb, trimmed and sliced thin
- 1 large carrot, shredded (can use prepackaged)
- 2 tablespoons sesame oil
- 1 bunch fresh mint, chopped
- 1 tablespoon sunflower oil
- 1 tablespoon soy sauce

Directions:

1. Combine the chopped cabbage, sliced fennel, shredded carrot, and chopped mint. Mix everything together thoroughly until the vegetables are well combined.
2. In a small bowl, whisk together the sunflower oil, sesame oil, and soy sauce until well combined.
3. Drizzle the oil mixture over the salad in the large mixing bowl.
4. Toss the salad gently to ensure that the vegetables are evenly coated in the dressing.
5. Serve the salad immediately, while it is still fresh and crunchy. Enjoy!

10. Bell Pepper Spiced-Sweet Tofu Bowl

Ingredients:

- 2 to 3 cups orange, red, or yellow bell peppers, stemmed, seeded, and diced
- 1 tablespoon coconut oil
- 3 garlic cloves, minced
- 1 (1-inch) ginger knob, minced
- 1 tablespoon turmeric
- 1 teaspoon red chili flakes
- 1 teaspoon sea or kosher salt
- 2 (14-ounce) packages firm tofu, drained and cubed
- ¾ cup coconut milk
- Juice of 1 lemon

Prep time

5 mins

Cook time

15 mins

Servings

2 - 4

Directions:

1. Heat the oil in a large skillet on a medium heat. Add the salt, chili flakes, turmeric, ginger, garlic, and oil.
2. Cook for six to eight minutes.
3. Stir in the tofu and peppers, and cook for 5 minutes.
4. After about 3 minutes, add the coconut milk and heat through.
5. Add lemon juice as a garnish and serve.

11. Turmeric and Lemon-Glazed Eggplant

Ingredients:

· 2 tablespoons turmeric

· 1 eggplant, diced

· 2 tablespoons ghee or coconut oil

· 2 tablespoons sea salt

· Squeeze of 1 lemon

Directions:

1. Salt the eggplant and place it in a sieve.
   Press out any extra liquid after letting it sit for 15 minutes.

2. Melt the ghee in a medium pan over medium heat.
   Add the ghee after adding the eggplant.

3. Cook the turmeric for 8 to 10 minutes after adding it.

4. Add the lemon juice and then serve.

Prep time

Cook time

Servings

2

12. Fiery Tomato and Chili Tofu

Ingredients:

- 2 to 3 cups chopped heirloom tomatoes
- 1 tablespoon coconut oil
- 3 garlic cloves, minced
- 1 (1-inch) ginger knob, minced
- 2 tablespoons turmeric
- 2 tablespoons ground coriander
- 2 tablespoons ground cumin
- 1 teaspoon sea or kosher salt
- 2 (14-ounce) packages firm tofu, drained and cubed
- Juice of 1 lemon
- 2 or 3 Thai chilies

Directions:

1. Heat the oil in a large skillet over medium heat.
   Add the salt, chili flakes, turmeric, ginger, garlic, and oil.

2. Cook for six to eight minutes.

3. Stir in the tofu and peppers, and cook for 5 minutes.

4. After about 3 minutes, add the coconut milk and heat through.

5. Add lemon juice as a garnish and serve.

Prep time

5 mins

Cook time

15 mins

Servings

2 - 4

13. Broccoli and Cauliflower Medley with a Twist

Ingredients:

- 1 head broccoli, chopped into florets
- 1 tablespoon minced fresh ginger
- 1 head cauliflower, chopped into florets
- 2 tablespoons turmeric
- 4 tablespoons olive oil
- 1 teaspoon sea or kosher salt

Directions:

1. Set the oven's temperature to 425°F.

2. In a big mixing bowl, combine the cauliflower florets and chopped broccoli, 1 teaspoon of salt, 2 tablespoons of turmeric, 1 tablespoon of minced fresh ginger, and 4 tablespoons of olive oil.
   Mix everything together thoroughly until the vegetables are well coated in the spices and oil.

3. Spread the broccoli and cauliflower florets out in a single layer on a baking sheet.

4. Place the baking sheet in the preheated oven and roast the vegetables for 15 to 20 minutes, or until they are golden brown and tender.

5. Once the vegetables are done roasting, remove the baking sheet from the oven.

6. Transfer the roasted broccoli and cauliflower to a serving dish and serve hot.

7. You can add additional salt and pepper to taste if desired.

Prep time

10 mins

Cook time

15 mins

Servings

4 - 6

The Ayurveda Cookbook for Women

14. Curry Leaf Tofu Stir-Fry

Ingredients:

- 5 curry leaves
- 2 (14-ounce) packages firm tofu, drained and cubed
- 1 tablespoon coconut oil
- 1 tablespoon turmeric
- 1 tablespoon paprika
- 1 tablespoon ground cumin
- Juice of 1 lemon
- ¼ teaspoon salt
- 1 (1-inch) ginger knob, minced
- 3 garlic cloves, minced
- 1 onion, sliced
- ½ cup toasted shredded coconut

Prep time

+ 10 mins
to marinate

Cook time

Servings

4 - 6

Directions:

1. To dry toast the coconut flakes, heat them in a small skillet over medium heat, stirring constantly until they turn golden brown, typically taking 1 to 2 minutes.
2. Marinate the tofu with the paprika, turmeric, cumin, lemon juice, and salt for 10 minutes in a small bowl.
3. Heat the oil in a big pan over medium heat, then add the onion, ginger, garlic, and curry leaves.
4. Cook for six to eight minutes.
5. Add the marinated tofu and continue cooking for an additional 5 minutes.
6. Add the coconut on top, then plate.

15. Mustard Seed and Curry Leaf Cauliflower

Ingredients:

- 4 tablespoons black mustard seeds
- 2 tablespoons sunflower oil
- 2 tablespoons curry powder (heat adjusted per dosha)
- 1 teaspoon sea or kosher salt
- 1 large head cauliflower, cut into florets (can use prepackaged)

Directions:

1. Heat the oil and mustard seeds in a big cast iron pan or wok over medium heat. Cook for 1 to 2 minutes, or until they pop.
2. Stir in the curry powder, then cook for one minute.
3. Add the salt and cauliflower, then toss to evenly distribute the hot oil over the florets.
4. Sauté for about 5 minutes, or until crisp-tender, and then serve.

Prep time

3 mins

Cook time

7 mins

Servings
2 - 4

16. Tofu and Greens Cherry-Almond Pilaf

Ingredients:

- 6 to 8 cups salad greens
- 1 tablespoon coconut, almond, or olive oil
- 1 cup chopped ripe cherries
- 1 cup chopped almonds
- 2 cups Israeli couscous
- 4½ cups vegetable broth
- 1 tablespoon freshly squeezed lemon juice
- ½ cup coconut milk
- 1 tablespoon ground fennel
- Pinch of salt
- 1 tablespoon ground cardamom
- ½ cup dried cherries
- ½ cup slivered almonds
- 2 (14-ounce) packages tofu, drained and cubed

Prep time

10 mins

Cook time

15 mins

Servings

6 - 8

Directions:

1. Heat the oil in a big saucepan. Cook the almonds and cherries for one minute after adding them.
2. Include the couscous and toast for two to three minutes.
3. Add the broth, bring to a boil, lower the heat to a low setting, and simmer, covered, for about 10 minutes, or until the liquid is absorbed.
4. Combine the coconut milk, lemon juice, fennel, cardamom, and salt in a big basin.
5. Add the tofu, couscous, almonds, and dried cherries and toss to incorporate.
6. Spoon the mixture over the lettuce.

17. Indian-Spiced Farmers' Market Veggies

Ingredients:

- 1 cup broccoli, chopped into florets
- 1 cup peas
- 1 cup cauliflower, chopped into florets
- 2 tablespoons fennel seeds
- 1 cup potatoes, diced
- 1 cup sweet bell peppers, stemmed, seeded, and chopped
- 2 tablespoons turmeric
- 4 tablespoons olive or sunflower oil
- 2 tablespoons ground coriander
- 1 teaspoon sea or kosher salt

Directions:

1. Set the oven's temperature to 425°F.

2. In a big mixing bowl, combine 1 cup of chopped broccoli florets, 1 cup of chopped cauliflower florets, 1 cup of peas, 1 cup of diced potatoes, 1 cup of chopped sweet bell peppers, 4 tablespoons of olive or sunflower oil, 2 tablespoons of turmeric, 2 tablespoons of ground coriander, 2 tablespoons of fennel seeds, and 1 teaspoon of sea or kosher salt.

3. Mix all of the ingredients together thoroughly until everything is well coated in the spices and oil.

4. Spread the broccoli-cauliflower medley mixture in a single layer on a baking sheet.

5. Place the baking sheet in the preheated oven and roast the vegetables for 15 to 20 minutes or until they are golden brown and tender.

6. Once the vegetables are finished roasting, remove the baking sheet from the oven.

7. Transfer the roasted broccoli-cauliflower medley to a serving dish and serve immediately.

Prep time

Cook time

Servings

18. Quinoa and Basil Thai Tofu Bowl

Ingredients:

- 1 (14-ounce) package firm tofu, drained and cubed
- 1 (15-ounce) can coconut milk
- 1 tablespoon coconut oil
- 1 teaspoon minced fresh ginger
- 1 cup quinoa
- 1 cup chopped toasted sunflower seeds
- 1 bunch fresh basil or Thai basil, chopped
- ½ cup soy sauce
- ¼ cup fresh mint, chopped
- ½ cup toasted shredded coconut

Prep time

8 mins

Cook time

22 mins

Servings

4 – 6

Directions:

1. To dry toast the coconut flakes, heat them in a small skillet over medium heat, stirring constantly until they turn golden brown, typically taking 1 to 2 minutes.

2. Combine the tofu and soy sauce in a small bowl.

3. Heat the oil in a big skillet. Sauté for two minutes after adding the ginger.

4. Add the tofu and cook for 5 to 6 minutes, or until it becomes brown.

5. Lower the heat to a low setting and stir in the quinoa, basil, and coconut milk. For 15 minutes, cook.

6. Add the coconut, mint, and sunflower seeds as garnish.

The Ayurveda Cookbook for Women

19. Lemon-Zested Spiced Potato and Spinach Dish

Prep time

5
mins

Ingredients:

- 4 large potatoes, diced
- 2 tablespoons ghee or sunflower oil
- 1 tablespoon turmeric
- 1 tablespoon ground coriander
- 2 tablespoons mustard seeds
- 3 garlic cloves, minced
- 1 large bunch spinach
- Juice and zest of 1 lemon
- 1 cup vegetable broth or water
- 1½ teaspoons sea or kosher salt

Cook time

25
mins

Directions:

1. Begin by melting 2 tablespoons of ghee in a large pan set over medium heat.

2. Once melted, add 2 tablespoons of mustard seeds to the pan and cook for 1 to 2 minutes or until the seeds start to burst.

Servings

4 - 6

3. Next, add 3 minced garlic cloves, 1 tablespoon of turmeric, and 1 tablespoon of ground coriander to the pan and cook for another 2 to 3 minutes.

4. Add 4 diced potatoes and 1 large bunch of spinach to the pan and cook for about 5 minutes or until the potatoes and spinach are tender.

5. Once the vegetables are cooked, add 1 1/2 teaspoons of sea or kosher salt, the juice and zest of 1 lemon, and 1 cup of vegetable broth or water to the pan.

6. Stir all of the ingredients together and allow them to cook for an additional 15 minutes.

7. Once the Spiced Spinach and Potato dish has finished cooking, it can be served immediately.

20. Broccoli and Tofu Sauté

Prep time

5
mins

Ingredients:

- 1 (14-ounce) package firm tofu, drained and cubed
- 2 cups broccoli florets (can use prepackaged)
- ½ cup soy sauce
- 1 tablespoon coconut oil
- 1 teaspoon minced fresh ginger
- 1 bunch fresh basil or Thai basil, chopped
- 1 cup chopped tomatoes
- ½ cup toasted sesame seeds

Cook time

10
mins

Directions:

1. For the toasted sesame seeds, dry toast them in a small skillet over medium heat until they turn brown, which should take about 1 to 2 minutes.

2. Combine the tofu and soy sauce in a small bowl.

Servings
2 - 4

3. Heat the oil in a large skillet over medium heat. Sauté for two minutes after adding the ginger.

4. Include the tofu and broccoli and sauté for 5 minutes.

5. Lower the temperature and stir in the basil. Until the basil wilts, cook for 1 to 2 minutes.

6. Add tomatoes and sesame seeds as a garnish.

7. Serve with quinoa, rice, or chapati or on its own.

21. Red Lentil and Spicy Potato Curry

Ingredients:

- 2 (14-ounce) cans coconut milk
- 3 potatoes, cubed
- 2 cups canned or fresh lentils
- ¼ cup tablespoons olive oil
- ¼ cup minced fresh ginger
- 3 tablespoons ground chili powder
- 6 garlic cloves, minced
- 3 tablespoon cumin seeds
- 3 tablespoon turmeric
- 2 large onions, sliced
- Juice of 1 lemon

Directions:

1. Boil the potatoes for 5 to 6 minutes in a big pan over high heat. Drain.
2. For 10 minutes, simmer the lentils with the coconut milk and ginger in a large saucepan over medium heat.
3. Heat the olive oil in a big pan over medium heat, then add the turmeric, cumin seeds, and chili powder. For one minute, cook.
4. Add the cooked potatoes, onions, and garlic and sauté for 10 minutes.
5. Combine the spice combination with the lentils and their broth.
6. Add lemon juice on top.

Prep time

Cook time

Servings

22. Swiss Chard and Pumpkin Seed Tofu Medley

Ingredients:

- 3 shallots, minced
- 3 tablespoons coconut oil
- 2 garlic cloves, minced
- 1 (14-ounce) package firm tofu, drained and cubed
- 1 tablespoon mild curry powder
- ½ cup toasted pumpkin seeds
- 3 cups stemmed and chopped Swiss chard
- Splash of vinegar or squeeze of 1 lemon

Directions:

1. Heat the oil in a large skillet over medium heat. Shallots, garlic, and curry powder are added, and they are sautéed for 2 minutes.
2. After adding it, simmer the tofu for 4 to 5 minutes.
3. Add the chard and simmer for three to five minutes.
4. Add the lemon juice and pumpkin seeds on top.
5. Put quinoa, rice, or chapati alongside.

Prep time

Cook time

Servings
2 - 4

The Ayurveda Cookbook for Women

23. Carrots with Lime, Raisins, and Mint

Ingredients:

- 6 to 8 carrots, peeled and grated (can use prepackaged)
- 2 handfuls fresh mint, chopped
- 1 cup raisins
- Juice of 1 lime
- 1 tablespoon honey

Directions:

1. Begin by peeling and grating 6 to 8 carrots into a large mixing bowl.

2. Add 1 cup of raisins and 2 handfuls of chopped fresh mint to the bowl.

3. In a small dish, combine the juice of 1 lime and 1 tablespoon of honey.

4. Drizzle the lime juice-honey mixture over the carrot-raisin-mint mixture in the large mixing bowl.

5. Mix all of the ingredients together thoroughly until they are well combined.

6. Serve the Carrot Raisin Salad immediately or chill it in the refrigerator until it's ready to be served.

Prep time

Servings

24. Tangy Tamarind Chickpea and Potato Curry

Ingredients:

- ¾ cup chopped fresh cilantro
- 3 potatoes, cubed
- ¼ cup sunflower oil
- 2 tablespoons cumin seeds
- 2 tablespoons turmeric
- 2 tablespoons ground coriander
- 1 tablespoon chili powder
- 2 onions, chopped

- 1 tablespoon fenugreek
- 1 (1-inch) ginger knob, minced
- 2 to 3 Thai chilies
- 2 (15-ounce) cans chickpeas, drained
- 2 to 3 tablespoons tamarind paste
- ¾ cup chopped fresh mint
- Squeeze of 1 lemon

Directions:

1. Boil the potatoes for 5 to 6 minutes in a big pan over high heat. Drain.

2. Add the chili powder, turmeric, cumin, coriander, fenugreek, and oil to a large pan and heat.

3. Prepare for one minute.

4. Cook the potatoes for 8 to 10 minutes after adding the onions, ginger, chiles, and tamarind.

5. Stir in the chickpeas and simmer for 4 to 5 minutes.

6. Add the lemon juice, mint, and cilantro over top.

7. Toss with tamarind chutney and serve over naan, quinoa, basmati rice, or chapati.

25. Corn and Pumpkin Seed Barley Bowl

Ingredients:

- 2 cups water
- ½ cup pearl barley
- ½ cup corn
- ½ cup quinoa
- ½ cup cannellini beans

- ¼ cup olive oil
- ¼ cup pumpkin seeds
- Squeeze of 1 lemon
- Freshly ground black pepper
- Sea salt

Directions:

1. Boil two cups of water in a medium saucepan.

2. Include the quinoa and barley and simmer for 15 to 20 minutes.

3. Quinoa and barley should be drained using a colander.
   Add the corn, beans, seeds, oil, and lemon back to the pan.

4. Toss, add salt and pepper, and then serve.

26. Cilantro-Kissed Spicy Chickpea Delight

Ingredients:

- 2 onions, chopped
- ¼ cup ghee
- 2 tablespoons turmeric
- 2 tablespoons ground coriander
- 2 tablespoons cumin seeds
- 1 tablespoon fenugreek
- 1 tablespoon garam masala
- 2 (15-ounce) cans chickpeas, drained
- Squeeze of 1 lemon
- 1 (1-inch) ginger knob, minced
- 1 cup water, divided
- ¾ cup chopped fresh cilantro

Directions:

1. Ghee should be heated in a big skillet. Cook for one minute after adding the turmeric, cumin, coriander, fenugreek, and garam masala.

2. Cook for 8 to 10 minutes after adding the onions and ginger.

3. Include the chickpeas in the pan. After 4 to 5 minutes of cooking, add the water in 1/4 cup batches to make a sauce.

4. Add the lemon and cilantro over top.

5. Combine with quinoa, chapati, naan, or basmati rice.

Prep time

Cook time

Servings
2 - 4

27. Garlicky Greens and Leftover Rice

Ingredients:

- 6 cups greens of your choice
- 3 tablespoons ghee
- 1 large onion, chopped
- 2 cups leftover wild, red, black, or basmati rice
- 5 to 6 garlic cloves, minced
- 1 teaspoon sea or kosher salt

Directions:

1. Melt the ghee in a large pan over medium heat, then add the onion and garlic.

2. Cook for about 5 minutes, or until browned.

3. Include the greens and cook for approximately 5 minutes.

4. Include the remaining rice and heat it through for 2 to 3 minutes.

5. Add salt to taste and then serve.

Prep time

Cook time

Servings
2 - 4

28. Ayurvedic Style Indian Cheese and Pea Curry

Ingredients:

- 2 cups chopped tomatoes
- ¾ cup raw cashews
- 2 large onions, sliced
- 3 tablespoons ghee
- ¼ cup minced fresh ginger
- 2 tablespoons ground coriander
- 1 tablespoon red chili powder
- 1 tablespoon ground cumin

- 1 tablespoon tomato paste
- 1 tablespoon turmeric
- 1 tablespoon ghee or olive oil
- 2 cups cubed paneer (packaged is fine)
- 1 tablespoon garam masala
- 1 cup fresh or frozen green peas
- 1 to 2 tablespoons coconut milk

Prep time

Cook time

Servings

4 - 6

Directions:

1. Grind cashews into a paste after soaking in boiling water (enough to cover) for 10 minutes.

2. Heat the ghee in a large pan over medium heat. Add the onions and ginger and cook for 2 minutes.

3. Include the turmeric, coriander, cumin, and chili powder. Add the tomatoes and tomato paste after 1 minute of sautéing. 5 minutes to cook.

4. In the meantime, cook the oil and paneer in a separate skillet over medium-high heat for 3 to 4 minutes, or until golden brown on both sides.

5. Stir in the coconut milk and garam masala after heating thoroughly, which takes around 2 minutes.

29. Cashew-Infused Minty Basmati Rice

Ingredients:

- 2 cups basmati rice
- ¼ cup coconut oil
- 1 handful fresh mint, chopped
- 1 cup chopped raw cashews
- 1 garlic clove, minced
- 4 cups vegetable broth
- 1 teaspoon salt

Directions:

1. Heat the coconut oil in a medium saucepan over medium heat. For 2 to 3 minutes, add the cashews, mint, and garlic.
2. After adding, boil the rice for 2 minutes.
3. Stir in the salt and broth, and then bring to a boil.
4. Lower the heat to low, cover the pot, and simmer for 15 minutes before serving.

30. Minty Spiced Coconut Lentil

Ingredients:

- 2 cups canned or fresh lentils
- 4 garlic cloves, minced
- 1 (14-ounce) can coconut milk
- 3 tablespoons olive oil
- 3 tablespoons minced fresh ginger
- 1 tablespoon ground chili powder
- 1 tablespoon turmeric
- 1 tablespoon cumin seeds
- 1 cup chopped fresh mint
- 2 large onions, sliced
- ½ cup toasted coconut flakes
- Juice of 1 lime
- 1 cup toasted cashews

Directions:

1. Spread the peanuts evenly in an ungreased pan and bake them in a preheated oven set to 350°F for roughly 15 minutes, making sure to stir them occasionally.
2. Place the coconut flakes in a small skillet and heat them over medium heat until they turn brown, which should take approximately 1 to 2 minutes, while stirring occasionally.
3. For 10 minutes, boil the lentils with the coconut milk and ginger in a large saucepan over medium heat.
4. Heat the olive oil in a big pan over medium heat, then add the turmeric, cumin, and chili powder. For one minute, cook.
5. After adding them, sauté the onions and garlic for 10 minutes.
6. Combine the spice combination with the lentils and their broth.
7. Add the cashews, lime juice, mint, and coconut flakes over top.

31. Cinnamon-Saffron Flavored Rice

Ingredients:

- 4 cups vegetable broth
- ¼ cup coconut oil
- 5 bay leaves
- 1 teaspoon saffron
- 8 cinnamon sticks
- 2 cups basmati rice
- 1 teaspoon salt

Directions:

1. The coconut oil should be heated in a medium saucepan over medium heat. Saffron, cinnamon sticks, and bay leaves should be added. 2-4 minutes of cooking time.

2. Include the rice, then cook for 2 minutes.

3. Bring to a boil after adding the salt and broth.

4. Lower the heat to a low setting, add a lid, and simmer for 15 minutes.

5. After serving, take the cinnamon and bay leaves out.

Prep time
3 mins

Cook time
19 mins

Servings
6 - 8

32. Lemon-Spiced African Quinoa

Ingredients:

- 3 cups vegetable broth
- 1 tablespoon sunflower oil
- 1 teaspoon freshly ground black pepper
- 2 teaspoons smoked paprika
- 1 teaspoon ground nutmeg
- 1 teaspoon ground cinnamon
- 1 teaspoon ground cumin
- 1 teaspoon ground cloves
- 3 tablespoons preserved lemon, minced
- 2 cups quinoa
- ¼ cup freshly squeezed lemon juice

Directions:

1. Warm up the sunflower oil in a medium saucepan. Cook for one minute after adding the smoked paprika, black pepper, nutmeg, cumin, cinnamon, and cloves.

2. Include the quinoa and toast it for two to three minutes.

3. Include the broth, lemon juice, and preserved lemon. Bring to a boil.

4. Lower the heat to a low setting and simmer the dish for 12 to 15 minutes with the lid on.

Prep time
5 mins

Cook time
20 mins

Servings
4 - 6

The Ayurveda Cookbook for Women

33. Indian Coriander Couscous Delight

Ingredients:

- 2 cups Israeli couscous
- 1 tablespoon sunflower oil
- 2 teaspoons ground cumin
- 1 tablespoon black mustard seeds
- 2 teaspoons turmeric
- 1 teaspoon fenugreek
- 1 teaspoon ground coriander
- 5 curry leaves
- 4½ cups vegetable broth

Prep time

Cook time

Servings

Directions:

1. Warm up the sunflower oil in a medium saucepan. Add the curry leaves, mustard seeds, cumin, turmeric, coriander, and other seasonings.

2. After one minute of cooking, stir in the couscous and toast for two to three minutes.

3. Include the broth and heat through.

4. Lower the heat to low and simmer for approximately 10 minutes, covered, to allow the liquid to be absorbed. Then, serve.

34. Sea Salt Roasted Chickpeas

Ingredients:

- 2 (15-ounce) cans chickpeas
- 1 tablespoon sunflower or coconut oil
- 1 tablespoon turmeric
- 1 tablespoon sea salt

Directions:

1. Set the oven to 450 degrees.

2. Combine the chickpeas, oil, turmeric, and sea salt in a medium bowl. Stir the chickpeas to evenly distribute the oil and seasonings.

3. Spread the chickpeas out on a medium pan and roast for 20 minutes. If the outside temperature is too high to put on the oven, they can instead be sautéed for 5 to 7 minutes on the stovetop.

Prep time

10 mins

Cook time

20 mins

Servings

4 - 6

The Ayurveda Cookbook for Women

35. Artichoke and Fried Sage Chickpea Medley

Prep time

2 mins

Ingredients:

- ¼ cup ghee
- 1 bunch sage leaves
- 2 (15-ounce) cans chickpeas, drained
- 2 (15-ounce) cans artichoke hearts, drained
- Squeeze of 1 lemon

Cook time

10 mins

Directions:

1. Heat the ghee and sage leaves in a large pan over medium heat. Cook until crispy for 3 to 4 minutes.

2. Transfer to a plate with a paper towel on top.

3. Stir in the chickpeas and artichoke hearts, and simmer for 4 to 5 minutes.

4. Transfer the chickpeas and artichoke hearts to a dish, garnish with the sage leaves, and then serve

Servings

4 - 6

36. Smoked Paprika-Spiced Black Bean Mash

Prep time

10 mins

Ingredients:

- 2 (15-ounce) cans black beans, drained
- ¼ cup freshly squeezed lemon juice
- ¼ teaspoon sea or kosher salt
- 4 to 6 garlic cloves, minced
- ¼ cup olive oil
- 3 tablespoons smoked paprika (or more to taste)
- Chopped scallions, for garnish

Servings

4 - 6

Directions:

1. Begin by opening the two cans of black beans and draining them.

2. Mash the black beans using a fork in a large mixing bowl.

3. Add 1/4 teaspoon of sea or kosher salt, 4 to 6 minced garlic cloves, 3 tablespoons of smoked paprika, 1/4 cup of freshly squeezed lemon juice, and 1/4 cup of olive oil to the bowl.

4. Mix all of the ingredients together until they are thoroughly combined.

5. Add chopped scallions as a garnish on top of the black bean mash before serving.

6. Serve the Black Bean Mash immediately, or chill it in the refrigerator until it's ready to be served.

37. Rosemary and Tomato Mediterranean White Beans

Ingredients:

- 2 (15-ounce) cans white beans, drained
- ¼ cup olive oil
- ¼ cup freshly squeezed lemon juice
- 4 to 6 garlic cloves, minced
- ¼ teaspoon sea or kosher salt
- 3 tablespoons chopped fresh rosemary
- Toasted pine nuts, for garnish
- Freshly ground black pepper

Prep time

10 mins

Servings

4 - 6

Directions:

1. Begin by opening the two cans of white beans and draining them.

2. In a large bowl, combine the drained white beans with 1/4 cup of freshly squeezed lemon juice and 1/4 cup of olive oil.

3. Add 4 to 6 minced garlic cloves, 3 tablespoons of chopped fresh rosemary, and 1/4 teaspoon of sea or kosher salt to the bowl.

4. Mix all of the ingredients together thoroughly until they are well combined.

5. Add freshly ground black pepper to taste.

6. Sprinkle toasted pine nuts on top of the bean mixture as a garnish.

7. Serve the Mediterranean White Beans with Rosemary immediately, or chill it in the refrigerator until it's ready to be served.

38. Scallion and Sesame-Flavored Red Bean Dish

Ingredients:

- ¼ cup freshly squeezed lemon juice
- 2 (15-ounce) cans red or adzuki beans, drained
- 1 garlic clove, minced
- ¼ cup olive oil
- 3 tablespoons toasted sesame seeds
- ¼ teaspoon sea or kosher salt
- ¼ cup chopped scallions
- Sesame oil, for garnish

Prep time

10 mins

Servings

4 - 6

Directions:

1. Start by opening the two cans of red or adzuki beans and draining them.

2. In a large bowl, combine the drained beans with 1/4 cup of freshly squeezed lemon juice and 1/4 cup of olive oil.

3. Add 1 minced garlic clove, 3 tablespoons of toasted sesame seeds, 1/4 cup of chopped scallions, and 1/4 teaspoon of sea or kosher salt to the bowl.

4. Mix all of the ingredients together thoroughly until they are well combined.

5. Add a small amount of sesame oil as a garnish to the top of the bean mixture before serving.

6. Serve the Red or Adzuki Beans with Sesame and Scallions immediately, or chill it in the refrigerator until it's ready to be served.

The Ayurveda Cookbook for Women

39. Olive and Sun-Dried Tomato Lentil Bowl

Ingredients:

- 2 cups Le Puy lentils
- 1 tablespoon sea or kosher salt
- 2 tablespoons turmeric
- 2 tablespoons freshly squeezed lemon juice
- ¼ cup olive oil
- ¼ cup tahini
- ¼ cup kalamata olives, chopped
- 1 cup chopped sun-dried tomatoes, drained of oil

Prep time

5 mins

Cook time

20 mins

Servings

4 - 6

Directions:

1. Fill a big saucepan halfway with water and bring it to a boil.

2. Add the 2 cups of lentils to the boiling water and cook for about 15 minutes or until they become soft. Once cooked, drain the lentils and allow them to cool.

3. In a medium bowl, combine 2 tablespoons of lemon juice, 1/4 cup of tahini, 1/4 cup of olive oil, 1 tablespoon of salt, and 2 tablespoons of turmeric.

4. Add the cooked and cooled lentils to the bowl, along with the chopped sun-dried tomatoes and kalamata olives.

5. Stir all of the ingredients together until they are thoroughly combined.

6. Once mixed, you can serve the lentil salad immediately or chill it in the refrigerator before serving.

Sides and Accompaniments

1. Fennel-Infused Carrot-Beet Yogurt Dip

Ingredients:

- ½ cup shredded carrot
- 2 cups plain Greek or regular yogurt
- ½ cup shredded fennel
- ½ cup shredded beets
- Pinch of sea or kosher salt
- 2 tablespoons chopped fennel fronds (optional)
- ¼ teaspoon ground coriander or fenugreek

Prep time

10 mins

Servings

6 - 8

Directions:

1. Combine the yogurt, carrot, beet, fennel, salt, and coriander in a medium bowl.
2. Combine thoroughly, if the mixture is too thick adding a tablespoon of water.
3. If using, garnish with fennel fronds before serving.

2. Radish-Cilantro Raita with a Kick

Ingredients:

- ¾ cup shredded carrot (can use prepackaged)
- 2 cups plain Greek or regular yogurt
- ¾ cup shredded radish
- ¼ teaspoon ground turmeric
- ¾ cup chopped fresh cilantro
- Pinch of ground cinnamon
- 1 to 2 tablespoons chopped fennel fronds
- Pinch of sea or kosher salt

Prep time

6 mins

Servings

6 - 8

Directions:

1. Combine the yogurt, carrot, radish, cilantro, turmeric, cinnamon, and salt in a medium bowl.
2. Combine thoroughly, if the mixture is too thick adding a tablespoon of water.
3. Add fennel fronds as a garnish and then serve.

3. Sweet and Spicy Ginger-Date Chutney

Ingredients:

- ¼ cup fresh ginger
- 2 cups fresh dates, pitted
- 1 to 2 tablespoons orange juice
- 1 teaspoon sea or kosher salt

Prep time

5 mins

Directions:

1. Blend the dates, ginger, orange juice, and salt in a blender.
2. If the mixture is too thick, add a little water or more juice.

Servings

6 - 8

The Ayurveda Cookbook for Women

4. Apple-Anise Chutney with a Mustard Seed Twist

Ingredients:

- 2 large onions, chopped
- 2 tablespoons sunflower oil or ghee
- 2 tablespoons minced mustard seeds
- ½ teaspoon ground allspice
- 1 tablespoon minced ginger

- 3 to 4 star anise
- 2 large apples, chopped
- 1 or 2 dried red chili peppers
- 1 teaspoon sea or kosher salt

Directions:

1. Heat the oil in a skillet over medium heat. After adding, sauté the onions for 5 minutes.
2. Add the ginger and mustard seeds, and heat for a further minute.
3. Add the salt, apples, chiles, star anise, and allspice. 20 minutes to cook.
4. Serve.

Prep time

3 mins

Cook time

26 mins

Servings

6 - 8

5. Tomato-Onion Tangy Chutney

Ingredients:

- 2 tablespoons minced fresh ginger
- 2 tablespoons sunflower oil or ghee
- 2 large ripe tomatoes, chopped
- 1 or 2 dried red chili peppers
- 2 large onions, chopped
- 1 tablespoon mustard seeds
- ¼ cup shredded coconut
- 1 tablespoon urad dal
- 1 teaspoon sea or kosher salt
- 2 curry leaves

Prep time

Servings

6 - 8

Directions:

1. Heat the oil in a skillet over medium heat. Ginger and chiles are added, and they are cooked for 2 to 3 minutes.

2. After adding them, simmer the tomatoes and onions for 10 minutes.

3. Combine the coconut, mustard seeds, urad dal, curry leaves, and salt with the tomato and onion combination in a blender and process until smooth.

4. If the texture is too thick, add a little water to thin it out to the right consistency.

5. Serve.

The Ayurveda Cookbook for Women

6. Cumin-Infused Garlicky Tahini Dressing

Prep time

5 mins

Servings

4 cups

Ingredients:

- 2 cups sesame oil
- 1 cup freshly squeezed lemon juice
- ¼ cup nut or seed oil
- ¾ cup tahini
- ½ cup soy sauce
- 5 garlic cloves
- 1 teaspoon sea or kosher salt
- 2 tablespoons mustard, mustard powder, or seeds
- 1 tablespoon ground cumin
- ¾ cup water
- ¼ teaspoon cayenne powder

Directions:

1. In a blender, combine the water, sesame oil, nut oil, lemon juice, soy sauce, tahini, mustard, garlic, salt, cumin, and cayenne until well-combined.

2. To change the consistency, add more tahini to make it thicker or more water or juice to make it thinner.

3. Serve as a dip with sides or on top of a salad.

7. Sesame-Ginger Vinaigrette

Prep time

5 mins

Servings

2 cups

Ingredients:

- 2 cups sesame oil
- 1 cup freshly squeezed lime juice
- ¼ cup olive oil
- ½ cup tamari sauce
- 1 teaspoon sea or kosher salt
- 2 tablespoons turmeric
- 3 garlic cloves
- 2 tablespoons ground ginger

Directions:

1. To make the sesame oil, olive oil, lime juice, tamari, garlic, turmeric, ginger, and salt smooth, combine them all in a blender.

2. Make any necessary seasoning adjustments and serve.

8. Lemony Yogurt Drizzle

Ingredients:

- 6 tablespoons olive oil
- ¾ cup Greek yogurt
- 3 tablespoons freshly squeezed lemon juice
- Zest of 1 lemon
- 1 tablespoon raw honey
- 1 to 2 tablespoons tahini
- 1 tablespoon turmeric
- 3 tablespoons water
- ½ tablespoon paprika
- Freshly ground black pepper
- Sea salt

Prep time

5 mins

Servings

4 - 6

Directions:

1. Combine the yogurt, oil, lemon juice, zest, tahini, honey, turmeric, paprika, and water in a blender and process until smooth.

2. Add salt and pepper to taste and serve.

9. Sun-Dried Tomato Walnut

Ingredients:

- 1 onion, diced
- 3 tablespoons olive oil
- ¼ teaspoon red chili flakes
- 5 garlic cloves, minced
- 2 (14-ounce) jars sun-dried tomatoes in oil, drained
- 1 cup chopped toasted walnuts
- 2 cups fresh Italian herbs, like basil, oregano, thyme, or sage
- Zest of 1 lemon
- Freshly ground black pepper
- Sea salt

Prep time

Cook time

Servings

Directions:

1. Heat the oil and onion in a large pan over medium heat. For two minutes, cook.

2. After cooking for 5 to 8 minutes, add the garlic and chili flakes.

3. Cook for a further 10 minutes before adding the sun-dried tomatoes, Italian herbs, and walnuts.

4. Add salt, pepper, and the zest as garnish before serving.

10. Creamy Avocado Sauce with a Citrus Zest

Ingredients:

- 4 garlic cloves
- 3 tablespoons freshly squeezed lemon juice
- 2 tablespoons olive oil
- ¼ teaspoon red chili flakes
- Zest of 1 lemon
- 2 avocados, peeled and pitted
- ¾ cup toasted pumpkin seeds or sunflower seeds (optional)
- Freshly ground black pepper
- Sea salt

Prep time

Servings

Directions:

1. Blend the garlic, oil, lemon juice, chile, and avocados in a blender until they are completely smooth.

2. Add 1 to 2 teaspoons of water to dilute the mixture if it is too thick.

3. Add the zest, seeds (if using), salt, and pepper, and then garnish before serving.

11. Vegan Garlic-Herb Alfredo

Ingredients:

- 2 garlic cloves, minced
- ¼ cup olive oil
  (or 1:1 olive oil and ghee)
- ¼ cup whole wheat flour
- 2 tablespoons chopped fresh basil
- 2½ cups almond milk
- 2 tablespoons chopped fresh parsley
- ¼ teaspoon ground nutmeg
- 2 tablespoons chopped fresh sage
- Freshly ground black pepper
- Sea salt

Prep time

Cook time

Servings

2 cups

Directions:

1. Heat the olive oil and garlic in a big pan over medium heat. For two minutes, cook.

2. Add the flour and mix it in until combined. For two minutes, cook.

3. Add the almond milk and stir until smooth.

4. After the sauce has reached a rolling boil, reduce the heat and stir in the basil, parsley, sage, and nutmeg.

5. Let the sauce simmer for five minutes.

6. Add salt and pepper to taste and serve.

12. Hearty Herbed Vegetarian Onion Gravy

Ingredients:

- 2 tablespoons plus ¼ cup ghee, divided
- ¼ cup barley flour
- 1 onion, diced
- 3 cups vegetable broth
- 2 tablespoons chopped fresh sage
- 2 tablespoons chopped fresh parsley
- 2 tablespoons chopped fresh thyme
- 2 tablespoons chopped fresh tarragon
- Freshly ground black pepper
- Sea salt

Prep time

Cook time

Servings

3 cups

Directions:

1. Melt 2 tablespoons of ghee in a large saucepan over medium heat. Add the onion. For 10 minutes, cook.

2. Stir in the flour after melting the last 1/4 cup of ghee. for three minutes.

3. Stir in the parsley, tarragon, sage, and vegetable broth.

4. Add salt and pepper to taste and serve.

The Ayurveda Cookbook for Women

13. Mango Salsa with a Cilantro-Mint Twist

Ingredients:

- 1 cup minced fresh cilantro
- 6 garlic cloves, minced
- 1 cup minced fresh mint
- 1 mango, peeled, pitted, and chopped
- ½ to ¾ cup olive oil
- ¼ to ½ cup minced fresh ginger
- Freshly ground black pepper
- Sea salt

Prep time

10 mins

Servings
2 cups

Directions:

1. Combine the cilantro, mint, garlic, mango, ginger, and olive oil in a medium bowl.
2. Add salt and pepper to taste and serve.

14. Almond-Cilantro Green Pesto

Ingredients:

- ¾ cup toasted almonds
- 3 garlic cloves
- 2 cups packed fresh cilantro leaves
- Juice of 1 lime
- 1 cup olive oil
- 1 teaspoon red chili flakes
- Freshly ground black pepper
- Sea salt

Prep time

5 mins

Servings
2 cups

Directions:

1. Blend the almonds, cilantro, garlic, lime juice, olive oil, and red chili flakes until smooth in a blender. Add water if it becomes too thick; if you're making pasta with this pesto, use the reserved pasta water.

2. Add salt and pepper to taste and serve.

Desserts and Sweet Treats

1. Lavender-Infused Coconut Bliss Bites

Ingredients:

- 1 cup unsweetened shredded coconut
- 1/4 cup coconut oil, melted
- 2 tbsp honey
- 1 tsp dried culinary lavender
- 1/4 tsp sea salt

Directions:

1. Combine the shredded coconut, melted coconut oil, honey, lavender, and sea salt in a food processor. Pulse until well combined and slightly sticky.

2. Using your hands, form the mixture into 12 small, round bites.

3. Arrange the bites on a plate lined with parchment paper. Refrigerate for 30 minutes or until firm. Enjoy chilled.

Prep time

15 mins

Cook time

0 mins

Servings
12

2. Cardamom-Scented Rosewater Panna Cotta

Ingredients:

- 2 cups coconut milk
- 1/4 cup honey
- 1 tsp ground cardamom
- 1 tbsp rosewater
- 2 tsp unflavored gelatin
- 1/4 cup cold water

Directions:

1. In a saucepan, heat the coconut milk, honey, cardamom, and rosewater over low heat until warm. Do not let it boil.

2. In a small bowl, dissolve the gelatin in cold water. Add the dissolved gelatin to the saucepan and stir well to combine.

3. Pour the mixture into 4 individual ramekins or dessert glasses. Refrigerate for at least 4 hours or until set.

4. Serve chilled, garnished with rose petals or chopped pistachios if desired.

Prep time

10 mins

Cook time

5 mins

Servings
4

The Ayurveda Cookbook for Women

3. Honey-Ginger Baked Apples with Cashew Cream

Ingredients:

· 4 large apples, cored

· 1/4 cup honey

· 1 tsp ground ginger

· 1/2 cup raisins

· 1/2 cup chopped walnuts

· 1 cup raw cashews, soaked for 4 hours and drained

· 1/4 cup water

· 1 tbsp honey

· 1 tsp vanilla extract

Prep time

Cook time

Servings

4

Directions:

1. Preheat your oven to 350°F (180°C).
   Place the cored apples in a baking dish.

2. In a small bowl, combine the honey, ground ginger, raisins, and walnuts.
   Stuff the apples with this mixture.

3. Bake the apples for 40 minutes or until tender.

4. While the apples are baking, prepare the cashew cream by blending the soaked cashews, water, honey, and vanilla extract in a food processor until smooth and creamy.

5. Serve the baked apples warm, topped with a dollop of cashew cream.

4. Lemon-Turmeric Quinoa Cookies

Ingredients:

- 1 cup cooked quinoa
- 1 cup almond flour
- 1/4 cup coconut oil, melted
- 1/4 cup honey
- 1 large egg
- 1 tsp grated lemon zest
- 1 tsp ground turmeric
- 1/4 tsp sea salt

Directions:

1. Preheat your oven to 350°F (180°C). Line a baking sheet with parchment paper.

2. In a large bowl, combine the cooked quinoa, almond flour, melted coconut oil, honey, egg, lemon zest, turmeric, and sea salt.

3. Scoop tablespoons of the mixture onto the prepared baking sheet, forming 12 cookies.

4. Flatten each cookie slightly with the back of a spoon.

5. Bake for 20 minutes or until the edges are golden brown. Allow the cookies to cool on the baking sheet for 5 minutes before transferring them to a wire rack to cool completely.

Prep time

20 mins

Cook time

20 mins

Servings
12

5. Ayurvedic Spiced Apple Crumble

Prep time

Cook time

Servings

Ingredients:

- 4 cups sliced apples
- 1/4 cup honey
- 1 tsp ground cinnamon
- 1/2 tsp ground cardamom
- 1/4 tsp ground nutmeg
- 1 cup rolled oats
- 1/2 cup almond flour
- 1/4 cup coconut oil, melted
- 1/4 cup chopped walnuts

Directions:

1. Preheat your oven to 350°F (180°C). Grease a 9-inch baking dish.

2. In a large bowl, combine the sliced apples, honey, cinnamon, cardamom, and nutmeg. Transfer the mixture to the prepared baking dish.

3. In another bowl, combine the rolled oats, almond flour, melted coconut oil, and chopped walnuts. Spread this mixture evenly over the apples.

4. Bake for 45 minutes or until the topping is golden and the apples are tender. Serve warm.

6. Chai-Spiced Poached Apricots with Almond Crumble

Prep time

Cook time

Servings
4

Ingredients:

- 12 dried apricots
- 1 1/2 cups water
- 1/4 cup honey
- 1 chai tea bag
- 1/2 cup almond flour
- 1/4 cup rolled oats
- 1/4 cup coconut oil, melted
- 1/4 cup chopped almonds
- 1/4 tsp ground cinnamon

Directions:

1. In a saucepan, combine the dried apricots, water, and honey. Bring to a gentle simmer.

2. Add the chai tea bag to the saucepan and let it steep for 5 minutes. Remove the tea bag and continue to simmer the apricots for an additional 15 minutes or until tender.

3. While the apricots are simmering, prepare the almond crumble by combining the almond flour, rolled oats, melted coconut oil, chopped almonds, and cinnamon in a small bowl.

4. Preheat your oven to 350°F (180°C). Spread the almond crumble on a parchment-lined baking sheet and bake for 10 minutes or until golden and crisp.

5. Serve the poached apricots warm, topped with the almond crumble.

7. Cherry-Ginger Chia Seed Parfait

Ingredients:

- 1 cup frozen cherries, thawed
- 1 tbsp grated fresh ginger
- 2 cups unsweetened coconut milk
- 1/2 cup chia seeds
- 1/4 cup honey
- 1 tsp vanilla extract

Directions:

1. In a blender, puree the thawed cherries and grated ginger until smooth. Set aside.

2. In a large bowl, whisk together the coconut milk, chia seeds, honey, and vanilla extract. Allow the mixture to sit for 10 minutes, stirring occasionally, until the chia seeds begin to thicken.

3. Divide the cherry-ginger puree among 4 parfait glasses or mason jars. Top each with an equal amount of the chia seed mixture.

4. Refrigerate the parfaits for at least 2 hours or until the chia seed mixture has thickened to a pudding-like consistency. 5. Serve the parfaits chilled, garnished with additional cherries or a sprinkle of coconut flakes, if desired.

Prep time

15 mins

Cook time

0 mins

Servings
4

8. Peachy Mint Compote

Ingredients:

- ¼ cup ghee
- 1 cup fresh mint leaves
- ½ cup water
- 3 cinnamon sticks
- 8 allspice berries
- 6 cloves
- 1 pound peaches, pitted and halved

Directions:

1. Bring the water, ghee, cinnamon, cloves, and allspice to a boil in a big pot.

2. Lower the heat, and let the mixture simmer for 5 to 10 minutes.

3. Add the peaches and stir. Cover and let stand for ten to fifteen minutes.

4. Eliminate the cinnamon sticks, add mint as a garnish, and serve.

Prep time

2 mins

Cook time

20 mins

Servings

6 - 8

9. Orange-Infused Brown Sugar Poached Pears

Ingredients:

- 2 cups plus 1 tablespoon orange juice, divided
- 6 pears, peeled, halved, and pitted
- 1 cup almond milk
- ¼ cup raw honey
- 1 tablespoon vanilla extract
- 1 teaspoon ground ginger
- ¼ cup brown sugar
- ¼ cup orange zest

Directions:

1. Bring the pears, 2 cups of orange juice, almond milk, honey, and brown sugar to a boil in a large saucepan over medium heat.

2. Include the remaining 1 tablespoon of orange juice together with the vanilla, ginger, and orange zest.

3. Simmer for 15 minutes with a lid on.

4. Serve.

Prep time

5 mins

Cook time

20 mins

Servings

6

10. Pistachio-Topped Saffron Carrot Pudding

Ingredients:

- 2½ pounds carrots, grated (can use prepackaged)
- ¼ cup sunflower oil
- 12 green cardamom pods, bruised
- 21 ounces almond milk
- 1 cup chopped pistachios
- ½ cup raw honey or maple syrup
- 1 to 2 tablespoons saffron

Prep time

5 mins

Cook time

25 mins

Servings

6 - 8

Directions:

1. Heat the oil in a big pot over medium heat. Add the carrots and simmer for 10 minutes.

2. Heat the almond milk, cardamom, pistachios, and saffron in a small saucepan over medium heat. Once the carrots are at the appropriate doneness, about 5 minutes later, reduce the heat to a simmer, cover, and put aside.

3. Add the cardamom to the carrots and boil for 10 minutes with the almond-saffron milk.

4. Add the honey and then serve.

11. Chocolatey Date Truffles

Ingredients:

- 2 cups almonds
- 2 cups dates, pitted
- 1 teaspoon vanilla extract
- 1 cup cacao nibs
- 1 tablespoon ground cinnamon
- Coconut oil, for blending (if needed)
- ½ cup cacao powder
- Almond or coconut flour, for blending (if needed)

Prep time

5 mins

Cook time

10 mins

Servings

2 - 4

Directions:

1. Boil the dates for 5 to 8 minutes over medium heat in a medium saucepan. Set alone for cooling.

2. Thoroughly combine the almonds, cacao nibs, cinnamon, and vanilla in a blender or food processor.

3. Include the dates and mix once more.

4. If the mixture is too dry, add the coconut oil. Add the almond flour if it's too moist or sticky.

5. Form into balls, then roll in cacao powder before serving.

12. Pepita-Coconut Energy Bites

Ingredients:

- ½ cup pumpkin seeds
- ½ tablespoon ground cardamom
- 1 cup shredded toasted coconut
- 2 tablespoons chia seeds
- 1 tablespoon raw honey or molasses
- ½ tablespoon ground cinnamon
- ¼ teaspoon salt
- Toasted pumpkin seeds (pepitas), for garnish
- ¼ cup coconut oil

7 mins

Cook time

15 mins

Servings
2 - 4

Directions:

1. To prepare the pumpkin seeds, spread them evenly in a pan and drizzle with either olive or coconut oil, making sure to coat them well by stirring. Next, place the pan in a preheated oven set to 350°F and bake for 5 to 15 minutes, depending on the size of the seeds, stirring every so often until they become golden brown.

2. Heat the coconut flakes in a small skillet over medium heat, stirring them continuously until they are toasted to a golden brown color, which should take approximately 1 to 2 minutes.

3. Combine the coconut oil, pumpkin seeds, chia seeds, cardamom, cinnamon, honey, and salt in a blender.

4. Form into balls, then roll or sprinkle in pepitas.

5. Keep chilled until you're ready to eat.

13. Creamy Almond Banana Ice Cream

Ingredients:

- 6 frozen bananas
- 1 cup chopped almonds

Prep time

3 mins

Servings
4 - 6

Directions:

1. Place the bananas in a food processor or blender and pulse until smooth.

2. Add the almonds on top before serving.

14. Blueberry-Fig Nutty Frozen Treat

Prep time
5 mins

Servings
2 - 4

Ingredients:

· 2 cups figs (fresh or frozen)
· 1 cup frozen blueberries
· ½ cup chopped almonds
· ½ cup almond butter (or 1 cup almonds)

Directions:

1. Whip the blueberries in a food processor or blender until they are smooth.

2. Blend in the almond butter and figs until well-combined.
   A tablespoon of water should be added if the mixture is too thick.

3. Add the almonds on top, then plate.

15. Saffron-Vanilla Seed Pudding

Prep time
25 mins

Servings
2

Ingredients:

· ½ cup chia seeds
· 2 cups coconut or almond milk
· 2 mashed bananas
· 3 tablespoons vanilla extract
· 1 teaspoon saffron
· ¼ teaspoon ground cinnamon

Directions:

1. Combine the coconut milk and chia seeds in a medium bowl.

2. Secondly, wait 20 minutes.

3. Include cinnamon, vanilla, saffron, and bananas.

4. Blend thoroughly, then serve.

The Ayurveda Cookbook for Women

16. Wild Berry Decadent Chocolate Seed Pudding

Ingredients:

- ½ cup chia seeds
- ½ cup slivered toasted almonds
- 2 cups almond milk
- ¼ cup cacao powder or nibs
- 1 to 2 cups berries of choice (strawberries, cherries, blueberries)
- 2 tablespoons raw honey

Prep time

25 mins

Cook time

7 mins

Servings
2

Directions:

1. Spread the walnuts evenly in an ungreased pan and place it in an oven preheated to 350°F. Toast the walnuts for 5 to 7 minutes, stirring occasionally, until they start to turn brown.

2. Combine the chia seeds and almond milk in a medium bowl. Wait 20 minutes.

3. Include the almonds, honey, cacao powder, and berries.

4. Blend thoroughly, then serve.

17. Creamy Chocolate Almond-Avocado Pudding

Prep time
10 mins

Cook time
3 mins

Servings
2 - 4

Ingredients:

- ¼ cup raw honey or molasses
- 2 avocados, peeled and pitted
- ¼ cup cacao nibs or powder
- 1 tablespoon vanilla extract
- ⅓ to ½ cup almond milk
- ½ teaspoon ground cardamom
- ½ cup shredded toasted coconut
- ½ teaspoon ground cinnamon

Directions:

1. Place the coconut flakes in a small skillet and heat over medium heat, stirring constantly until they turn brown, which should take around 1 to 2 minutes.

2. Puree the avocados, almond milk, vanilla, cardamom, and cinnamon in a blender until smooth.

3. Add the coconut on top before serving.

18. Cinnamon-Orange Basmati Rice Pudding

Prep time
3 mins

Servings
2 - 4

Ingredients:

- 1 cup almond milk
- 1 cup leftover cooked basmati rice
- Peels of 1 to 2 oranges
- 2 tablespoons cinnamon
- 1 to 2 vanilla beans, split lengthwise

Directions:

1. Combine the rice and almond milk in a medium bowl.

2. Garnish with orange peels, vanilla beans, and cinnamon before serving.

19. Almond-Spiced Pumpkin Pudding

Ingredients:

- 2 cups almond or coconut milk
- 1 (14-ounce) can pumpkin purée
- ¼ cup chia seeds
- ¼ cup almond butter
- 1 cup chopped figs or dates
- 1 tablespoon vanilla extract
- 1 teaspoon ground allspice
- 1 tablespoon raw honey
- 1 teaspoon ground ginger
- ¼ teaspoon sea or kosher salt
- 1 teaspoon ground cloves

Directions:

1. Blend or stir the pumpkin, almond milk, chia seeds, figs, almond butter, vanilla, honey, allspice, ginger, cloves, and salt in a blender or mixing bowl until thoroughly combined.

2. To set, chill for 20 minutes.

3. Serve.

Prep time

Cook time

Servings

4

Ayurvedic Beverages

1. Spiced Warm Milk

Ingredients:

· 8 ounces of whole organic milk
· A tiny pinch of dried ginger (optional)
· A tiny pinch of cinnamon (optional)

Directions:

1. Pour the whole organic milk into a microwave-safe drinking mug.

2. Add a tiny pinch of cinnamon and a tiny pinch of dried ginger, if desired. Stir.

3. Microwave the milk for 20-30 seconds. Depending on the power of your microwave, cooking time may vary.

4. Stir the milk once more to make sure that the spices are well combined.

Prep time

1 mins

Cook time

30 secs

Servings

1

2. Pomegranate Aloe Lime Drink

Ingredients:

- 1 cup of pomegranate juice
- 2 teaspoons of turbinado sugar
- 1 tablespoon of aloe vera gel
- 1 fresh lime

Directions:

1. Juice the lime and set the juice aside.

2. In a glass, combine the pomegranate juice, turbinado sugar, and aloe vera gel. Mix until the sugar is mostly dissolved.

3. Add the lime juice and stir to combine.

4. Serve the drink in a chilled glass with a slice of lime for garnish.

Prep time

5 mins

Cook time

0 mins

Servings

1

3. Watermelon Lime Cardamom Smoothie

Prep time
5 mins

Ingredients:

· 1/8 teaspoon of ground cardamom
· 2 cups of fresh watermelon cubes, seeds removed
· 2 wedges of fresh lime

Cook time
0 mins

Directions:

1. Remove all seeds from the watermelon cubes.
2. Place the watermelon cubes into a blender. Squeeze the lime wedges over the watermelon.
3. Sprinkle ground cardamom over the top of the watermelon.
4. Puree the ingredients until smooth.
5. Serve the watermelon lime cardamom smoothie in a chilled glass, with a lime slice garnish.

Servings
1

4. Cardamom-Fennel-Mint Infused Water

Prep time
5 mins

Ingredients:

· 1/2 cup of fennel seeds
· 8 cups of water
· 1/2 cup of cardamom seeds
· 1 handful of mint

Cook time
5-10 mins

Directions:

1. In a large pot, bring the water to a boil.
2. Add the fennel seeds, mint, and cardamom seeds, and turn off the heat.
3. Steep the ingredients as the water cools.
4. Once the water has reached room temperature, strain the ingredients and discard them.
5. Serve the Cardamom-Fennel-Mint Infused Water in a glass filled with ice.

Servings
1

5. Rose-Fennel-Clove Infused Water

Ingredients:

· 1 handful of rose petals
· 8 cups of water
· 1/4 cup of red cloves
· 1/2 cup of fennel seeds

Directions:

1. In a medium pot, bring the water to a boil.
2. Add the fennel seeds, rose petals, and red cloves, and turn off the heat.
3. Steep the ingredients as the water cools.
4. Once the water has reached room temperature, strain the ingredients and discard them.
5. Serve the Rose-Fennel-Clove Infused Water in a glass filled with ice.

Prep time
5 mins

Cook time
5-10 mins

Servings
1

6. Lemon-Saffron Sweet Tea

Ingredients:

· 5 cups of water
· 1/4 teaspoon of saffron
· 1 tablespoon of cardamom seeds
· 1 tablespoon of raw honey
· 1 tablespoon of fennel seeds
· Zest of 1 lemon

Directions:

1. In a medium pot, bring the water, cardamom seeds, saffron, fennel seeds, and lemon zest to a boil.
2. Boil the mixture for 5 minutes, then remove from heat and let it sit for another 5 minutes.
3. Stir in the raw honey and serve the Lemon-Saffron Sweet Tea.

Prep time
3 mins

Cook time
10 mins

Servings

2 - 4

7. Cumin-Cilantro Rose Tea

Ingredients:

- 5 cups of water
- 1/4 cup of fresh cilantro leaves
- 3 tablespoons of cumin seeds
- 3 or 4 rose petals

Directions:

1. In a medium pot, bring the water, cumin seeds, rose petals, and cilantro leaves to a boil.

2. Boil the mixture for 5 minutes, then remove from heat and let it sit for another 5 minutes.

3. Strain the tea into cups and serve the Cumin-Cilantro Rose Tea.

Prep time

3 mins

Cook time

10 mins

Servings

2 - 4

8. Ginger-Basil Sparkling Water

Ingredients:

- 1 (2-inch) ginger knob, peeled
- 1 Lemon Juice
- 8 cups of sparkling water (can use flavored)
- 1/8 to 1/4 cup of raw honey, depending on your taste
- Fresh basil sprigs, for garnish

Prep time

5 mins

Servings

1

Directions:

1. In a blender, blend the lemon juice, ginger, and honey until well combined.

2. Pour a few tablespoons of the mixture into a glass, then fill the glass with the sparkling water.

3. Adjust the mixture to taste, and garnish with fresh basil sprigs.

4. Serve the Ginger-Basil Sparkling Water in a glass filled with ice.

9. Spiced Turmeric-Pepper Tea

Ingredients:

- 5 cups of water
- 1 tablespoon of cardamom seeds
- 1 (2-inch) ginger knob, peeled
- 1 tablespoon of black peppercorns
- 1 teaspoon of turmeric
- 1/4 teaspoon of saffron
- 2 tablespoons of cloves
- 1 tablespoon of raw honey

Prep time

8 mins

Cook time

10 mins

Servings

2 - 4

Directions:

1. In a medium pot, bring the water, ginger, cardamom seeds, black peppercorns, saffron, turmeric, and cloves to a boil.

2. Boil the mixture for 5 minutes, then remove from heat and let it sit for another 5 minutes.

3. Stir in the raw honey and serve the Spiced Turmeric-Pepper Tea.

10. Almond Cinnamon Chai

Ingredients:

- 4 cups of water
- 4 cloves
- 6 crushed cardamom pods
- 3 star anise pods
- 1 (1-inch) ginger knob
- 2 cinnamon sticks
- Pinch of salt
- 1 teaspoon of raw honey
- 1 cup of almond milk

Prep time
8 mins

Cook time
10 mins

Servings
1

Directions:

1. In a medium pot, bring the star anise, water, ginger, cardamom, cloves, cinnamon, and salt to a boil.

2. Boil the mixture for 5 minutes, then remove from heat and let it sit for another 5 minutes.

3. Stir in the almond milk & honey, and strain the Almond Cinnamon Chai into a cup.

The Ayurveda Cookbook for Women

11. Spiced Honey Anise Chai

Ingredients:

- 6 crushed cardamom pods
- 4 cups of water
- 4 cloves
- 2 cinnamon sticks
- 1 (1-inch) ginger knob
- 3 star anise pods
- 1 tablespoon of fennel seeds
- 1 cup of almond milk
- 1 teaspoon of black tea
- 1 teaspoon of raw honey

Prep time

Cook time

Servings

1

Directions:

1. In a medium pot, bring the water, cloves, cardamom, star anise, ginger, cinnamon, fennel seeds, and black tea to a boil.

2. Boil the mixture for 5 minutes, then remove and let it sit for another 5 minutes.

3. Stir in the honey and almond milk, and strain the Spiced Honey Anise Chai into a cup.

12. Vanilla Cacao Chai

Ingredients:

- 1 or 2 vanilla beans
- 4 cups of water
- 1 cinnamon stick
- 1 tablespoon of fennel seeds
- 6 crushed cardamom pods
- 1 cup of coconut, rice, soy, or hemp milk
- 3 tablespoons of cacao nibs

Prep time
8 mins

Cook time
10 mins

Servings
1

Directions:

1. In a medium pot, bring the water, vanilla, cardamom, cinnamon, and fennel seeds to a boil.

2. Boil the mixture for 5 minutes, then remove and let it sit for another 5 minutes.

3. Stir in the cacao nibs and coconut milk, and strain the Vanilla Cacao Chai into a cup.

13. Minty Mango Smoothie

Ingredients:

- 1 mango, peeled and pitted
- 1 handful of fresh mint
- 1 cup of plain or soy yogurt
- 3 cups of water

Prep time
3 mins

Servings
2

Directions:

1. In a blender, blend the yogurt, mango, water, and mint until it becomes a smooth mixture.

2. Pour the smoothie into 2 glasses and serve the Minty Mango Smoothie.

The Ayurveda Cookbook for Women

14. Ginger Lime Yogurt Drink

Prep time

2 mins

Ingredients:

- 1/4 cup of organic whole milk yogurt
- 1 cup of room temperature water
- 1-inch piece of fresh gingerroot, peeled and coarsely chopped
- Juice of 1/2 small lime
- 1 teaspoon of raw honey (optional)

Servings

2

Directions:

1. Using a hand blender or carafe blender, blend together the yogurt, water, fresh ginger, lime juice, and honey (if using) on high speed for 1-2 minutes until it becomes a smooth mixture.

2. Pour the Ginger Lime Yogurt Drink into 2 glasses and serve.

15. Spiced Ginger Digestive Tea

Prep time

2 mins

Ingredients:

- 2-3 black peppercorns
- 2 cups of water
- 1/2-star anise
- 1/2-inch piece of fresh gingerroot, coarsely chopped (including the skin)
- 2-3 cloves
- 1/2 teaspoon of ground cinnamon

Cook time

10 mins

Directions:

1. In a small saucepan, bring 2 cups of water to a boil.

2. Coarsely chop the gingerroot, with the skin, and add it to the boiling water along with the star anise, cloves, peppercorns, and cinnamon powder.

3. Reduce the heat to low and let the mixture simmer for 10 minutes or longer.

4. Strain the Spiced Ginger Digestive Tea into 2 mugs.

5. Drink 6 ounces of the tea either with or after meals to aid digestion.

Servings

2

Conclusion

As we reach the conclusion of The Ayurveda Cookbook for Women 2024, it is my hope that you have discovered the immense potential of Ayurveda to transform your health, well-being, and overall quality of life. By incorporating the principles of this ancient wisdom into your daily routines and culinary choices, you are taking a proactive and empowered approach to nurturing your body, mind, and spirit.

Throughout this book, we have explored the fundamental concepts of Ayurveda, delved into the art of Ayurvedic cooking, and provided you with over 150 nourishing and delectable recipes designed specifically for women. By now, you should have a solid understanding of how Ayurveda can support your unique constitution, and how to adapt your diet and lifestyle to achieve balance, harmony, and optimal wellness.

As you continue on your Ayurvedic journey, remember that it is a lifelong process of self-discovery, growth, and transformation. Be patient with yourself and embrace the changes as they unfold. You may find that your tastes and preferences evolve over time, reflecting the shifts in your physical, emotional, and spiritual well-being. This is a natural part of the journey and a testament to the dynamic nature of Ayurveda.

I encourage you to continue exploring the world of Ayurveda, seeking out new knowledge, ingredients, and techniques to further enrich your understanding and practice. Connect with like-minded individuals, seek guidance from Ayurvedic practitioners, and immerse yourself in the vibrant global community of Ayurvedic enthusiasts. Your curiosity and dedication to personal growth will serve you well on this path.

Remember that the ultimate goal of Ayurveda is to cultivate a deep sense of harmony and contentment within yourself and with the world around you. As you embrace this ancient wisdom, you will inevitably find that it permeates every aspect of your life, infusing it with a sense of balance, peace, and joy that transcends the kitchen and nourishes your soul.

Thank you for allowing me to be your guide on this transformative journey. I wish you a lifetime of health, happiness, and culinary adventures as you continue to embrace the Ayurvedic way of life. May the wisdom of this ancient tradition bring you abundant blessings, and may your newfound knowledge serve as a beacon of light, illuminating the path to your highest potential.

Made in the USA
Las Vegas, NV
04 January 2024

83910664R00083